The Modern University

The Modern University
A MODEL ORGANIZATION

A. K. RICE
With a Foreword by Lord Fulton

TAVISTOCK PUBLICATIONS
London · New York · Sydney · Toronto · Wellington

First published in 1970
by Tavistock Publications Limited
11 New Fetter Lane, London EC4
This book is set in Bembo 12 on 13 point
and was printed in Great Britain
by The Camelot Press Limited
London and Southampton
© *The Tavistock Institute of Human Relations, 1970*

SBN 422 73470 5

Distributed in the United States of America
by Barnes & Noble, Inc.

Contents

		page
	FOREWORD by Lord Fulton	vii
1	INTRODUCTION	1
2	A SYSTEM THEORY OF ORGANIZATION	7

The enterprise as an open system – Boundary controls – Sentient systems – Organizational models – Multiple-task systems – Temporary and transitional task systems – Transactional task systems

3	UNIVERSITY OBJECTIVES	20
4	ORGANIZATIONAL MODEL FOR TASK PERFORMANCE: RESEARCH	26

The classification of research work – Scientists as the throughput – Problem-centred research – Research-programme management – Specialization – An organizational model for university-based research

5	ORGANIZATIONAL MODEL FOR TASK PERFORMANCE: EDUCATION	41

The operating systems of education – The integration of learning – Growth and maturation

6	A MODEL ORGANIZATION FOR UNDERGRADUATE EDUCATION	56

The activities of undergraduate education – University expansion – The case for research at undergraduate level – A model organization for an undergraduate educational institution

7	POSTGRADUATE EDUCATION	71

Research – Professional training

CONTENTS

		page
8	A MODEL ORGANIZATION FOR A UNIVERSITY The problem of size	81
9	SOME MAJOR CONSTRAINTS ON TASK PERFORMANCE Participation in decision-making – The dependent culture of the educational process – Tenure – The university and its society – The explosion of knowledge – The sophisticated demands of society – The decline in religious belief – Standards of scholarship	88
10	UNIVERSITY GOVERNANCE The role of vice-chancellor – Governance	102
11	CONCLUSION	107
	INDEX	111

Foreword
Lord Fulton

The author of this book was for long associated with the Tavistock Institute of Human Relations, and his death last year came as a grievous blow. He has drawn on his experience of universities in a number of countries in three continents; he was professionally eminent in the study of the ways in which men organize themselves to achieve different kinds of tasks and purposes. His assessment of the maladies that have beset universities in recent years is sharp, and should be uncomfortable, even disturbing, reading for the over-complacent.

Ken Rice brought to his analysis of university organization a training in social diagnosis. He took the view that while universities must accept a measure of responsibility for their present plight they are perhaps more sinned against than sinning; for they have been asked in recent times to undertake successively tasks that are complex, numerous, and not easily to be reconciled with one another. So tensions have been built up of a kind common to universities everywhere.

Many of those who know our own universities will go a long way with this reading of their situation. Relations, for instance, between junior and senior members; between the humane and the scientific studies; between pure and applied in teaching and research; between the impinging market forces of the outside world and the traditional 'parity of esteem' among all academic disciplines – these and other sources of tension are in part at least the consequences of new functions thrust on the universities since the war. Before 1939, for example, our universities, as teaching institutions, were almost exclusively engaged in educating the scholars of the next generation and those who were destined for the practice of the learned professions. Some 50,000 university places were sufficient for that broad purpose. Now, the places number 225,000 and by 1980 it is estimated that there will be approximately 450,000. This is not a matter only of size: it is a new commitment. Already the larger part of the student population is destined not for scholarship or the learned professions but for the world of action and affairs. The problem grows more urgent of how and what to teach in undergraduate courses that will satisfy the needs, not only of those who are going on through postgraduate courses to prepare for careers in scholarship, but also of those who go straight from their undergraduate studies into public affairs, into industry, commerce, communications, management, and so forth.

The task of the universities could doubtless be simplified by the provision of different kinds of institution for the different needs; but there would be many who would deeply regret the loss of mutual understanding, which is the reward of educating together at the undergraduate stage the future scholar and the future man of affairs.

Rice has chosen, as his method, to examine separately each of the different tasks inherent in the objectives of the university; and subsequently to offer a model organization best suited for the performance of those tasks, taking into account that they are in reality interdependent. He offers, finally, reflections on the control and government of the proposed organization.

He did me the honour of asking me to read a draft of his book and to comment on it. He was cut off before we could meet to discuss it. For my part, I would have acknowledged the importance of his 'task analysis'. The universities have their obligations to society and must find the organization best fitted fully to discharge them at the lowest social cost. But I would have wished to ask, first, whether a model organization based exclusively upon the analysis of identifiable, definable tasks (e.g. the production of highly trained manpower) does not run the risk of converting the universities into no more than instruments; and, second, for an expansion of the account of the 'sentient group'. Was he here touching on the concept of the university as a society lit by its own vision of the good life: a way of living that captures for good some of those who join as undergraduates; and that gives to those who leave at the end of three years some insights that permanently enrich their work in the world outside? Must we believe that this view of the university has been altogether lost in growth, size, complexity, and the accelerated pace of life?

The author's views on these questions can be only surmised. That they should arise from the reading of his book would surely have pleased him.

CHAPTER I

Introduction

When I was in India in the autumn of 1968 I had the opportunity to look at, and to think about, some of the problems of university organization.[1] Indian universities, like those in other parts of the world, were upset by student unrest. Some were closed entirely, others kept working spasmodically, and still others appeared to require almost as many police as faculty members in order to remain open. It seemed to me then, as now, that what the students were protesting about at any one time, in any particular university, was less important than that they were protesting; and that, though the protests in different countries, and in different universities in the same country, often had widely different objectives, there were two common factors in every case: first, the protesters were all young; and, second, the protests were all against the 'establishment'.

We, who are now old, protested when we were young. We believed that our elders, who composed the then 'establishment', had caused the first world war and had thus jeopardized our futures. But we did not prevent the second. Not only that, but we produced a technological, political, and social system whose destructive capacity we no longer seem able to control. It is hardly surprising that the young of today should not trust us. They protest because they believe that if affairs are left in our hands they will not have any future at all.

This theme has been widely discussed. The origins and course of protests in America, Europe, and Asia have been studied and compared. The difficulty is that such diagnoses so often leave a sense of impotence in the face of the immensity of the changes that are required: nothing less than a revolution of the economic system and a destruction of the vested interests that support the existing value

---

[1] The members of the group with whom I worked and to whom I owe thanks were Professors K. Chowdry, I. Dayal, R. Matthai, R. Shah, and A. Turner, and Messrs. Kakar and Parikh.

systems. I cannot help feeling that such discussions, and the statements that result,[1] while being insightful and accurate, nevertheless help to avoid taking a cold hard look at what is immediately practical in the universities themselves. For there is another common factor: student protests are often directed against their own universities, and those who manage them.

It has already become fashionable in many countries to lay the blame on a 'comparatively small group of militants' who lead the riots and organize the 'sit-ins'; and to assert that they are anti-authority of any kind. It may even be comforting to university officials to believe that they are not the real targets of protest, but simply the available ones. But before we accept such generalizations it might be wise to examine just what are the tasks of a contemporary university, how they have changed, and what, if anything, there might be in the university system itself that makes it so vulnerable to and deserving of attack.

In earlier times, when, by today's standards, universities were comparatively small, enclosed communities of scholars, there appears to have been little doubt about university objectives – the discovery and dissemination of knowledge. Members of the faculty and their students found less difficulty in communicating with each other. Even so, students were known to riot. Today, the enormously increased demand for higher education, the explosion of knowledge, and the social misgivings about the use to which the knowledge is being put, have not only thrown doubt on university objectives but made meaningful communication between faculty and students difficult, and, in many universities, apparently impossible.

In India, during the past twenty years, there have been two international commissions, and a large number of committees appointed by the government, to report on university and other kinds of education. All of them have recommended change. The last, the Education Commission 1964–66, opened its report thus:

'The destiny of India is now being shaped in her classrooms. This, we believe, is no mere rhetoric. In a world based on science and technology, it is education that determines the level of prosperity, welfare and security of the people.'

---

[1] For example, G. Wald, quoted in the *New Yorker*, 22 March 1969.

INTRODUCTION

The report concludes:

'The stakes are too big to be taken lightly. We trust that to this tremendous challenge there will be an adequate response.'

Throughout its report the commission deplores how little study has been made of many organizational problems, and how little notice has been taken of earlier reports and recommendations.

Since that report was issued it has become increasingly clear, not only that students have become more vociferous in their protests, but that they are frequently joined by members of the faculty who themselves complain of inadequate communications with university management. Even in countries with a far longer university tradition than India, the problems of university governance need urgent attention.

I had been working for many years with my colleagues in the Tavistock Institute on a system theory of organization;[1] we had applied it in a variety of settings, both industrial and non-industrial. The aim of this short book is to examine what light this theoretical framework casts on university problems and on the difficulties of implementing organizational change.

My starting-point is a brief examination of the objectives and goals of university institutions. From that point, however, rather than try to examine existing organizations in any detail, and to understand how they do, or do not, provide adequate machinery for attaining the goals, I try to define the actual tasks that have to be performed and to analyse the systems of activity that are essential for task performance. Thereafter I suggest model organizations that stem from the analysis. I accept that this is a theoretical exercise, and that even if one were starting with a 'green-field site' – green not only in having neither buildings nor faculty, but in having neither tradition nor culture to contend with – it would hardly be possible to implement the models without compromise. Nevertheless I hope that the attempt may serve to clarify some of the assumptions and myths that lie behind contemporary difficulties and conflicts.

My justification for this approach is that I cannot believe that the

[1] A. K. Rice, *Productivity and social organization*, 1958; A. K. Rice, *The enterprise and its environment*, 1963; E. J. Miller and A. K. Rice, *Systems of organization*, 1967 (all Tavistock Publications, London).

many able men and women who staff and manage the universities of the world could have allowed the present situation to arise were it not for the existence of very powerful, but unrecognized, social forces that inhibit change and maintain the chaos. It seems to me preferable, then, to examine the tasks and organizational implications before considering how they are currently performed. So often, consideration of current performance degenerates into a process of apportioning blame for failure, whereas organizational analysis frequently demonstrates that the existing organization does not allow, let alone facilitate, competent performance. Indeed, it often appears that the organization is designed to prevent it.

A central concept used in the analysis is that of the *primary task*. This is defined as the task that any institution or sub-institution must perform if it is to survive. The concept is related to a theory of organization that treats any institution or sub-institution as an open system, that is, a system that depends for its existence on a continuous exchange of materials with its environment. The first theme of this book is that universities are multiple-task institutions; and that each task, though interdependent with other tasks, requires its own characteristic organization which differs from the organization required for other tasks and for the whole. The second theme is that concentration on the interdependence of the tasks has tended to obscure their independent values, with consequent confusion of tasks, boundaries of activity systems, roles, and role relationships. In effect, because of expansion the 'community of scholars' has become differentiated into a number of sub-communities with diverse and often conflicting interests. The third theme is that present university organization is based for the most part on closed-system characteristics, in which transactions with the environment are kept to a minimum. But the day is past when a university could dictate its requirements to its society, and, having acquired them, could retire into its ivory tower, content that it could pay its debts over a long term. Society now demands attention to its contemporary problems, and a much quicker pay-off for its investments.

In his report to the Yale Corporation for the year 1967-68, the President, Kingman Brewster, wrote:

'Yale and every other university badly needs a theory, or at

INTRODUCTION

least a way of thinking about its function, which will tell itself, and explain to others, what the University should and should not try to do in the application of its tangible resources and its know-how to the solution of social problems.'

I have no such theory. But I try to demonstrate that, under today's conditions, universities have no alternative but to come to terms with the societies in which they exist. They have to preserve standards of scholarship, but they have to apply them to the unstable and violent present, lest they not be allowed to survive to preserve the past. Some traditions will have to go.

I take the view that a university is a complex multiple-task enterprise, which, to perform its many tasks, has to relate to a complex environment. The environment includes its local community, its catchment areas for faculty and students, its state or nation, and the reference groups that pass judgement on its academic status. Elite universities have major international relationships as well. Their activities are intricate and interrelated. For such a complex institution there can be no simple organization. The future organization, however reached, will always have to be complex. The only hope, so far as I can see, is that, with more precise definition of the boundaries of activity systems, and of the boundary controls these entail, it will become possible to identify roles, responsibilities, and authorities more easily; and that, with more sophisticated role behaviour, it will become possible to control transactions across the boundaries more effectively. But even this will not be enough: knowledge is advancing too rapidly, and technology is changing societies too quickly. The future organization must also, therefore, be sufficiently flexible to be able to evolve as knowledge increases. Organizational change has to become a continuous process.

Chapter 2 summarizes the concepts and assumptions used in the analysis. Chapter 3 discusses briefly current definitions of the objectives of universities, and attempts definitions of the multiple tasks that have to be performed in order to achieve the objectives. In Chapters 4 and 5 model organizations are described for the two major task systems: research and education. Chapter 6 combines these into one model. In Chapter 7 some of the problems of postgraduate education, both the teaching of research and professional education, are taken up. Then in Chapter 8 a model organization for a university is put forward. Chapter 9 considers the major constraints on university task performance, with examples taken from different cultures. Chapter 10 discusses university governance. The final chapter suggests a possible pilot experiment.

CHAPTER 2

A System Theory of Organization

THE ENTERPRISE AS AN OPEN SYSTEM

The theory treats any enterprise or institution, or a part of any enterprise or institution, as an open system. Such a system must exchange materials with its environment in order to survive. The difference between what it imports and what it exports is a measure of the conversion activities of the system. Thus a manufacturing company imports raw materials, converts them, and exports finished products. For the outputs it receives a pay-off, from which it acquires more intakes. The intakes into the teaching system of a university are students; and the outputs graduates (and failures). Provided the quality of its outputs (graduates) is maintained, the university continues to receive resources and to attract students.

Such intakes and outputs are the results of import-conversion-export processes that differentiate enterprises from each other. Every enterprise has a variety of import-conversion-export processes: a manufacturing company, for example, recruits employees, assigns them to jobs, and sooner or later exports them through retirement, resignation, dismissal, or death. It imports and consumes power and stores; it collects data about markets, competitors, and suppliers' performance, and converts the data into plans, designs, and decisions about products and prices.

The nature of the many processes and their intakes and outputs reveals the variety of relationships that an enterprise, or part of it, makes with different parts of its environment, and, within itself, between its different parts. The processes also reveal the variety of tasks that the enterprise performs as a whole, and the contributions of its different parts to the whole. Every enterprise, or part-enterprise, has, however, at any given time, a primary task – the task it must perform if it is to survive.[1] The dominant import-conversion-export

[1] For a fuller description of this concept and the system theory of organization, see Miller and Rice, op. cit.

process is that process by which the primary task is performed. And it is the dominant process that defines the essential relationship of an enterprise to its environment, and to which other relationships, tasks, and throughputs are subordinate.

BOUNDARY CONTROLS

A *system of activities* is that complex of activities that is required to complete the process of transforming an intake into an output. A *task system* is a system of activities plus the human and physical resources required to perform the activities. The term 'system', as it is used here, implies therefore that each component activity of the system is interdependent with at least some of the other activities of the same system, and that the system as a whole is identifiable as being in certain, if limited, respects independent of related systems. Thus a system has a boundary which separates it from its environment. Intakes cross this boundary and are subjected to conversion processes within it. The work done by the system is therefore at least potentially measurable by the difference between its intakes and its outputs.

What distinguishes a system from an aggregate of activities is the existence of regulation. Regulation relates activities to throughput, ordering them in such a way as to ensure that the process is accomplished, and that the different import-conversion-export processes of the system are related to each other, and the system as a whole to its environment.

Consequently, the most important *management* control in any organization is the control of the boundaries of systems of activity, since it is only at boundaries that the difference between intake and output can be measured. Task management, then, is essentially:

(a) the definition of boundaries between task systems;
(b) the control of transactions across boundaries.

The boundary of a system of activities therefore implies both a discontinuity and the interpolation of a region of control. The location of the boundary control function is shown in *Figure 1*.

A SYSTEM THEORY OF ORGANIZATION

Those systems of activity that lie in the mainstream of the dominant import-conversion-export process, through which the primary task is performed, are the operating systems. Where in any enterprise there is more than one operating system, a differentiated managing

FIGURE 1 *A task system and its boundary control function*

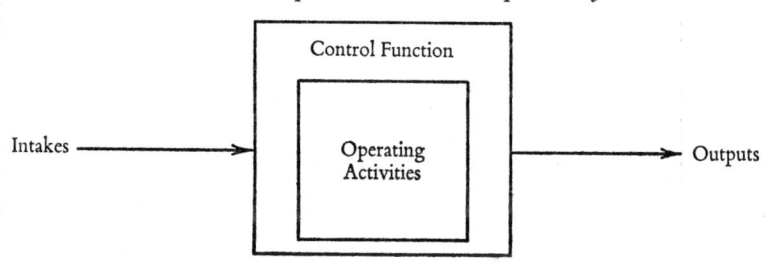

system is required to control, coordinate, and service the activities of the different operating systems. This will include the management of the total system, management of each discrete operating system, and also management of those non-operating systems that do not perform directly any part of the primary task of the whole, but that provide controls over, and services to, the operating systems. An enterprise with three first-order operating systems, three control and service functions in the first-order managing system, two second-order operating systems, and two second-order control and service functions, is shown in *Figure 2*. In it, to avoid complexity, the topological form of *Figure 1* has been simplified by locating the boundary control region at one point on the boundary of the operating system (see *Figure 1a*).

FIGURE 1a *Simplification of previous figure*

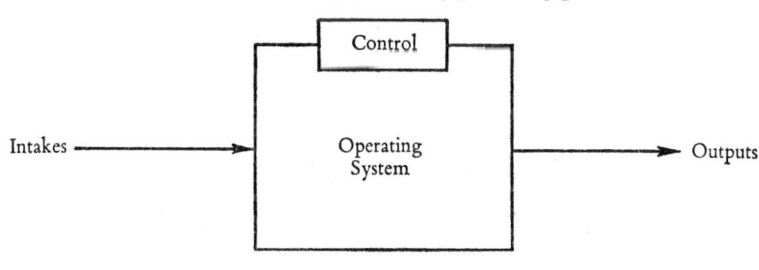

FIGURE 2 *Organizational model*

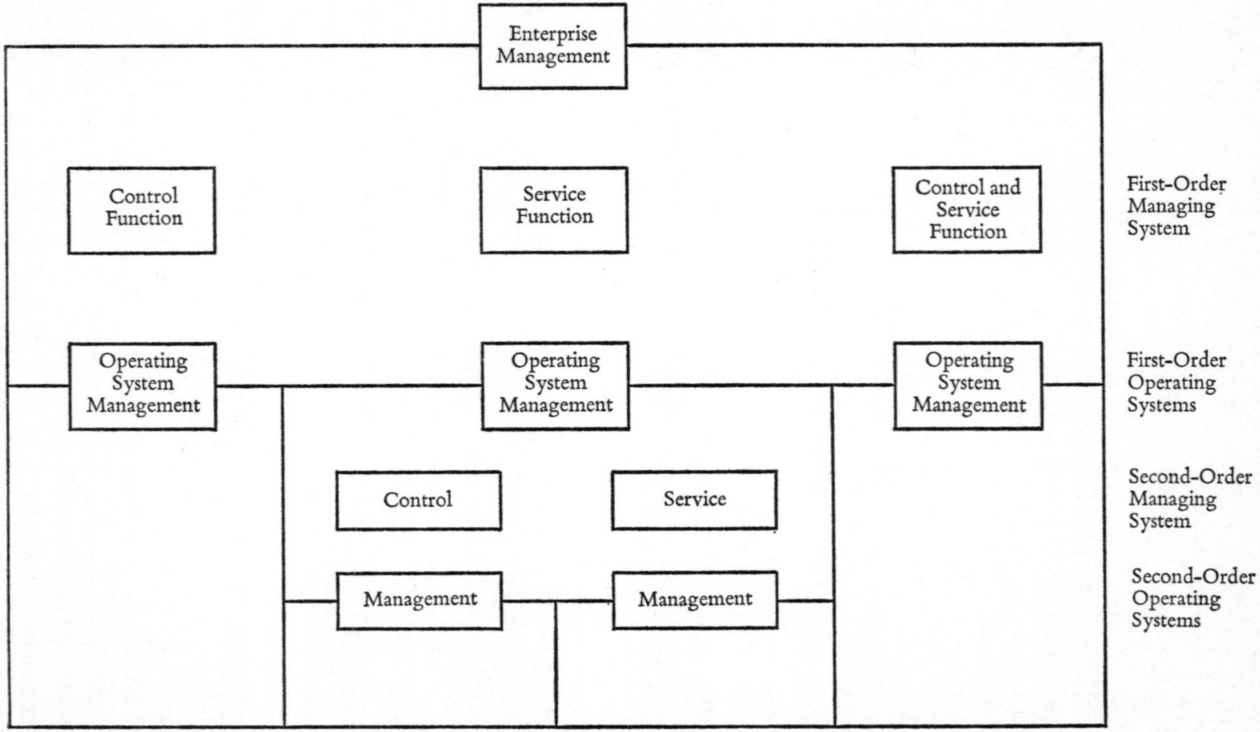

SENTIENT SYSTEMS

Members of an enterprise occupy roles in these various systems of activity. One member may take more than one role; and one role may be taken by more than one member. In assigning activities to roles and roles to persons, the enterprise cannot always predetermine that each individual will commit himself wholeheartedly either to the role and tasks to which he has been assigned or to the other members of his task system. The individual may indeed give his loyalty to other groups in the enterprise – to his union, to his friends, to colleagues doing the same kind of job in other task systems; or he may give it to groups outside the enterprise – to his family, to his religion, or to his political party. The enterprise, in other words, cannot predetermine the relative *sentience* of the various groups to which each individual will belong. These memberships are nevertheless relevant to the effectiveness of task performance, supporting or opposing it.

Management of an enterprise requires, therefore, three kinds of boundary control:

> (a) regulation of task-system boundaries (i.e. regulation of the whole enterprise as an import-conversion-export system, and regulation of constituent systems of activity);
>
> (b) regulation of sentient-system boundaries (the boundaries of the groups to which individuals belong, either directly through their roles in systems of activity or indirectly through their consequential role-sets and personal relationships);
>
> (c) regulation of the relation between task and sentient systems.

ORGANIZATIONAL MODELS

Organization is the instrument through which an enterprise assigns activities to roles and roles to individuals and groups. Organization is thus a means to an end, and the most appropriate organization is the one that best fits primary-task performance. It follows that for every task an organizational model is required, which will define the boundaries of operating systems and the control and service functions that are required to coordinate, control, and service them. Such definitions of the boundaries of the systems will determine the roles and role relationships that provide for effective performance.

In building an organizational model, the starting-point is the process flow. The dominant process identifies the nature of the intakes, the activities required to convert these into, and dispose of, outputs, and the human and physical resources required to provide or to facilitate these activities. The next step is to discover the discontinuities in the process that mark the boundaries of systems of activity. These are the appropriate points at which to draw organizational boundaries, and these in their turn define management commands.

Since the performance of any task is subject to complex constraints, the actual organization of the enterprise will inevitably be a compromise between the model and the constraints. In the same way, since each part of any enterprise has its own primary task and thus requires an organizational model for itself, the organization for the whole will be constrained by the need to integrate the organizations of the parts. The model provides a basis against which to examine the reality of the constraints and the consequent compromises.

Thus to the three boundary controls given above there must be added a fourth: the regulation of organizational boundaries where these, because of unalterable constraints, do not coincide with the boundaries of activity systems.

Task, organizational, and sentient boundaries may coincide. Indeed, they must coincide to some extent at the boundary of the enterprise if it is to continue to exist. The enterprise may also be differentiated into parts, which are similarly defined by coinciding boundaries. There are dangers in such coincidence. One danger is that members of a group may so invest in their identity as a group that they will defend an obsolescent task system from which they derive membership. One can add the possibility that the identification of change in task-system boundaries, and even the identification of the boundaries themselves, can be made difficult by the existence of group boundaries that are strongly defended.

In general, it can be said that, without adequate boundary definitions for activity systems and sentient groups, organizational boundaries are difficult to define and frontier-skirmishing is inevitable. It is perhaps a major paradox of modern complex enterprises that the more certainly boundaries can be located, the more easily can formal communication systems be established. Unless a boundary is adequately located, different people will draw it in different places and hence there will be confusion between inside and outside. In the individual this confusion leads to breakdown; in enterprises to inefficiency and failure.

Because an enterprise is an open system, the nature of the constraints within which it operates is constantly changing. Internally, a change in technology may remove old constraints and introduce new ones. Externally, changes may range from a minor statutory requirement to a major shift in the definition of the primary task. Such changes, even if they do not demand a redefinition of the primary task of the whole, frequently redefine the primary tasks of parts and modify the strategies through which an enterprise relates its internal and external environments so as to achieve the most effective performance of its primary task. Changes in strategy may not always be explicit; they may be merely reflected in changes in the behaviour of the enterprise. Different forms of organization differ in their capacity to respond and adapt to changes in strategy. Strategic changes, whether or not they are explicit, and even if they do not entail a redefinition of the primary task, may require changes in the form of organization if this is to retain its effectiveness.

MULTIPLE-TASK SYSTEMS

A simplified form of a multiple-task system is shown in *Figure 3*. Theoretically, two tasks, and thus two systems of activity, can be identified, but those who perform the tasks – the human resources of the two systems – constitute a single, and identical, sentient group. Thus the strength of the sentient boundary of the group is affected by what happens in both activity systems, and, by way of the common sentient group, the activities of each task system are affected by those of the other. Involvement of a group in two activity systems may require the coexistence of two different arrays of roles and role relationships – arrays that may relate the individual members together in different ways.

System conflict does not arise in conditions of stable equilibrium – in other words, where environmental forces are tenuous or do not impinge too differentially on the three systems. For example, primitive societies often seem to have had relatively closed-system characteristics over a long time. A stable equilibrium was established between the different systems of activity in which the tribal group engaged. But in contemporary society, with its increasingly rapid social and technological change, disequilibrium is common.

FIGURE 3 *One group – two task systems*

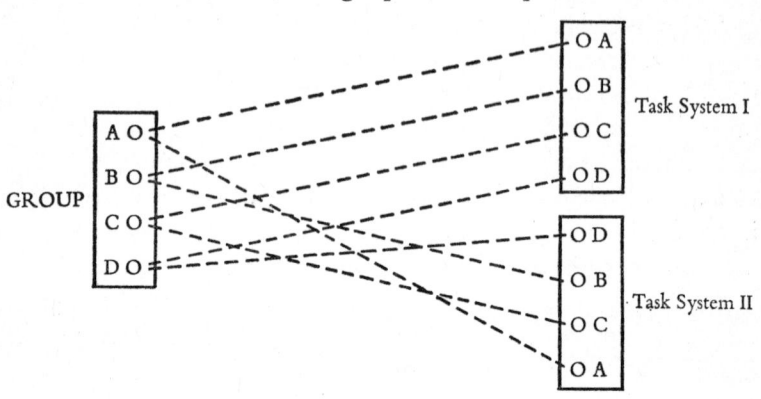

Family businesses provide many examples of disequilibrium because of the differential pressures on the different systems of activity: those pertinent to the family as a family, and those pertinent to the business as a business. In the kind of business that requires increasing capital to maintain parity with competitors, it is difficult for any but the most wealthy family to provide enough to maintain control. If, in addition, the business requires increasing numbers of technicians, scientists, and managers to handle the more sophisticated technologies of production, marketing, and control, it is unusual for one family to be able to provide them all. As others outside the family are introduced into positions of power in the business task system, they tend to usurp the expected roles of family members, and thus distort role relationships in the family system.

In conditions of social and technical change, the attitudes and behaviour of members of a group to each other, and to the external environment, may not only jeopardize the survival of the task systems but put such strain on internal group relationships that group survival is also jeopardized.

TEMPORARY AND TRANSITIONAL TASK SYSTEMS

By definition, temporary and transitional task systems require temporary and transitional organizations (for convenience, called *project organizations*). The essential feature of a project type of organization is that the group brought together to perform a particular task has to be disbanded as soon as the task is completed. The group as a group has no further *raison d'être* in terms of task performance. But the theoretically finite life of a project team is frequently prolonged as a result of a redefinition of its task or of the accretion of new tasks. A research team, for example, either because it has invented a new technique or because its members have become devoted to working together, generates further problems to which it can apply its technique, or which will keep the team intact – irrespective of whether the generated problems are relevant to the overall task of the research enterprise of which the team is a part.

But project groups cannot by definition provide either permanent sentience or career patterns for their members. Or, if they do, they become difficult to disband at the conclusion of task performance. A successful project-type organization requires, therefore, control and service functions in the managing system:

(a) to ensure that adequate resources, both human and physical, are available for every project undertaken;

(b) to provide sentient groups to which members can commit themselves and to which they can return for reallocation at the conclusion of each project;

(c) to provide pools in which physical resources can be stored and maintained.

The general form of organization is illustrated in *Figure 4*. In a small enterprise, the total enterprise can be the only sentient system required. But a large and complex enterprise can seldom provide sufficient personal identity, and separate differentiated systems are then essential.

FIGURE 4 *The general form of a project organization*

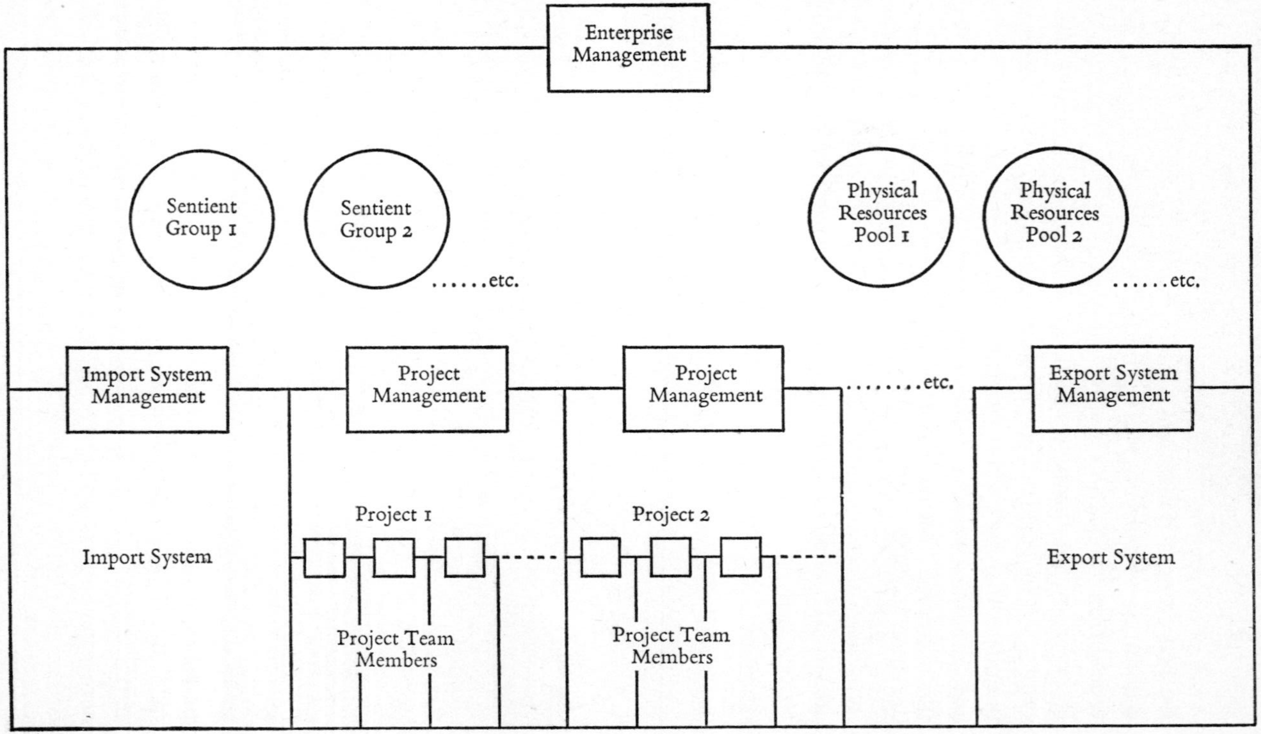

TRANSACTIONAL TASK SYSTEMS

By definition, a transaction between an enterprise and its environment must take place across the boundary of the enterprise. The activities of the transaction involve those parts of the enterprise and of its environment through which the transaction is made. The task system of the transaction, however temporary, has, therefore, a boundary that cuts across enterprise boundaries, a boundary that in any genuine two-way transaction cannot be fully controlled by the enterprise. Moreover, if the enterprise is large, not all of its members can take part in the transaction and one or more have to 'represent' the enterprise. This condition inevitably involves the control of boundaries between the enterprise and its representative or representatives.

FIGURE 5 *A simple transactional task system*

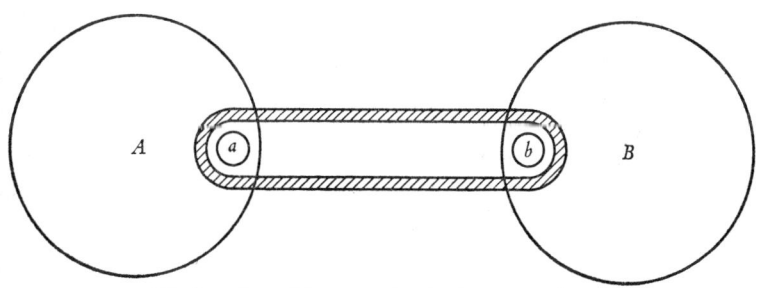

The boundary of the transactional task system is shaded

A simple example is illustrated in *Figure 5*, which represents a transaction between two enterprises *A* and *B*; *a* conducting the transaction on behalf of *A*, and *b* on behalf of *B*. For the duration of the transaction the task-system boundary (*ab*) cuts across the enterprise boundaries of both *A* and *B*. In so far as there is any uncertainty in *A, B, a, b,* or *ab* about the relative strengths of the *A, B, a, b,* or *ab* boundaries, there will be doubts about the control of transactions across the boundaries between *A* and *a*, *B* and *b*, and *a* and *b*. Control of the *ab* boundary must be strong enough to perform the task of transaction, but it must not become too strong, for then it will jeopardize control of the *Aa* and the *Bb* boundaries, and hence the integrity of the A and B boundaries. Any uncertainty can be exacerbated when either a or b consists of more than one individual. Then not only may there be uncertainty about the Aa and Bb boundaries but the intragroup relations of a and b may also cause anxiety.

Examples of difficulty are common. If a is a sales representative of a supplier A and b is the buyer of a customer B, the management of A will require its representative a to make a good relationship with b, and at the same time to remain loyal to A. A representative who is suspected of favouring b at the expense of A does not usually last long. Similarly, a buyer who is believed to use the ab relationship for his own benefit rather than for the benefit of B gets short shrift as soon as he is caught. In the same way, negotiations between groups acting on behalf of institutions, or even nations, may create uncertainty about control of the boundaries of the institutions they represent; furthermore, different opinions among the delegates of the negotiating groups about the task they are engaged on can threaten the whole transaction.

Some transactions by their nature give power and privilege to one party to the transaction. Most such transactions are governed by social and even legal sanctions. If A in *Figure 5* represents the medical profession and a a member of it, and B represents the community and b a patient, then very strict rules, with legal backing, govern the nature of the transactions and the role relationships within the task-system boundary. Other professions have equally strict rules. But even in transactions in which no recognized professions are involved, the ab boundary (the control region of which is shaded in *Figure 5*) is usually 'controlled' by cultural conventions to which both A and B subscribe. In the absence of such conventions, or in default of acceptance of recognized conventions, much time and effort have to be spent in establishing rules and procedures before performance of the real transaction can start.

More generally, any transaction between an enterprise and its environment introduces some uncertainty as to the relative strengths of the boundaries of the enterprise, the environment, and the transactional task system. If chaos is defined as uncertainty about boundary definition, or, more colloquially, as not knowing who or what belongs where, then every transaction is potentially chaotic. If we go further and suggest that the major characteristic of disaster is the obliteration of known boundaries (of the guides and directories that govern existence), then every transaction can be said to have built into it the elements of incipient disaster. The doctor who has sexual intercourse with his patient – that is, who allows personal relationships in the task-system boundary to obliterate the boundary of the medical profession to which he belongs – is, in reality, courting disaster.

The transactional task system is temporary and transitional. When the task has been performed it should be discontinued. If it is prolonged beyond task completion, it uses resources unnecessarily. By so doing it must reduce the efficiency of task performance. It requires, therefore, a project-type organization which may or may not be renewed.[1]

At the end of the transaction a is once more enclosed in A, and b in B. But whatever the outcome of the transaction, the relationships of a to other parts of A and to the whole A (and of b to B) are likely to have changed. And it is at this stage that any disagreements within a (or b) are likely to affect the formation of future 'project teams' for transactional tasks.

The general point is that, in terms of its transactions with the environment, an enterprise is a multiple-task system, forming temporary project teams (of one or more members) for task performance, and subsequently disbanding them. For the duration of the transaction a project team operates with the authority of the enterprise. Every transaction tests the integrity of the boundaries of the enterprise and of the project team, and the integrity of the control that the enterprise can exercise over its own project team – that is, over the extent to which the project team acts at the level of authority it has been given, or above or below that level. The outcome of every transaction can thus change the nature and strength of the controls.

The common defences against uncertainty of control are the precise definition of terms of reference for the project team and the prescription of rules and procedures for dealing with any unforeseen or unplanned activities in the transaction. But the defences, by adding constraints to the transactional task system, must put limits on performance.

[1] In this conceptual framework the calls made by a sales representative are seen as separate 'projects'; between calls he 'returns' to his sentient group within his company.

CHAPTER 3

University Objectives

In his convocation address to the University of Allahabad in 1947, just after Indian independence, Pandit Nehru defined university objectives thus:

> 'A university stands for humanism, for tolerance, for reason, for progress, for the adventure of ideas, and for the search for truth. It stands for the onward march of the human race towards even higher objectives. If the universities discharge their duty, then it is well for the nation and the people.'

The report of the Indian Education Commission 1964–66 defines the objectives as:

> 'to seek and cultivate new knowledge, to engage vigorously and fearlessly in the pursuit of truth, and to interpret old knowledge and beliefs in the light of new needs and discoveries;
>
> to provide the right kind of leadership in all walks of life, to identify gifted youth and help them to develop their potential to the full by cultivating physical fitness, developing the powers of the mind, and cultivating right interests, attitudes and moral and intellectual values;
>
> to provide society with competent men and women trained in agriculture, arts, medicine, science and technology, and various other professions, who will also be cultivated individuals, imbued with a sense of social purpose;
>
> to strive to promote equality and social justice and to reduce social and cultural differences through the diffusion of education;
>
> to foster in the teachers and students, and through them in society generally, the attitudes and values needed for developing "the good life" in individuals and society'.

UNIVERSITY OBJECTIVES

This long definition is coloured by what the members of the Commission saw as some of the immediate problems bedevilling progress towards 'the good life' in contemporary India. Nevertheless, apart from some changes in emphasis, I believe there are few in university governance who would quarrel with the broad principles behind these two definitions. Even protesting students would, I believe, accept that if only truth were vigorously and fearlessly pursued, appropriate reforms would follow.

A major difficulty of all these definitions is that they assume that knowledge, its discovery and acquisition, is in itself good. I am not arguing that it is not; but that there are many people in the world today, particularly the young, who are deeply concerned about the use to which knowledge, especially in science and technology, is put. Or perhaps it would be more correct to say that they are disturbed and angry at the uneven advance of knowledge – the lag of the behavioural as compared with the natural sciences – and at the exploitation of science and technology at the expense of human values. The 'explosion' of knowledge of recent years has made communication between members of different academic disciplines difficult enough, if not, as some claim, already impossible. The student eager to learn and to apply the learning to the problems of mankind is confronted by an increasing array of specializations, whose adult advocates bicker and fight with each other over what the student can only feel to be trivial issues, largely irrelevant to any value system that gives human welfare and development a high priority. It is, perhaps, small wonder that, all over the world, students feel they are being let down by their educational systems and are trying to find other, more humane, values by which to order their lives.

At the same time, in both the developed and the developing countries, the demand for opportunities for higher education is increasing at a rate with which existing institutions cannot cope. In some countries the demand is from the young, who know, or believe, that higher education leads to better careers; in others, the primary demand is from society, for more qualified scientists and technologists. In most countries these demands reinforce each other. In a few affluent countries, higher education often seems to be provided less for its own sake than as a means of occupying, for ever-longer periods of time, a growing and articulate part of the population whose members cannot be absorbed into the existing economic system; at least, not at the levels at which their education warrants and at the age at which they could make an important contribution to social wellbeing.

But it seems to me that the basic dilemma is the conflict of cultural values. The exploitation of modern science and technology entails discarding the older in favour of the newer, not only with regard to material artifacts but with regard to emotional and religious values as well. Modern technology is directed towards increased mastery of the environment; modern science towards more factual and reality-based explanations of natural phenomena, including human life and death. The exploitation of modern science and technology means accepting the values of competition and aggression. The old and those who cling to it must be discarded in favour of the new and those who advocate it. Modern knowledge challenges traditional beliefs. The conflict is between modern knowledge, with its inescapable competitive and destructive values, and traditional knowledge, with its very different and often deeply rooted religious values. The dilemma is universal, but perhaps in India, with its great traditions and classical culture, it can be seen in more acute form. There are, I believe, many Indians, including advocates of progress, who have a deep and largely unrecognized horror of the values that appear always to accompany the acquisition of modern knowledge. They are distressed at their inability to reconcile the obvious need to alleviate the ills of their society by the application of technology with the effects of the latter on their cultural heritage. Socially, this leads, in India, as among the youth of most countries, to an unconscious, and often conscious, contempt for modern science and scientists. The trend away from science and technology and back to the arts is no accident.

India is one of the uncommitted nations of the world. Perhaps it is uncommitted in more than a political sense: it is uncommitted to the rat race that appears, at present, the inevitable concomitant of a modern technological society. More knowledge may, or may not, allow mankind to benefit from the knowledge and yet avoid the rat race. More knowledge may, or may not, lead to mastery of the environment without making the environment increasingly impossible to live in. Experience so far suggests that more knowledge only increases competitiveness and destructiveness.

One of the ironies of the present student protest movement is that many of those it attacks, the officials and senior faculty members of the universities, are upholders of the values to which the protesters would themselves subscribe. The protests, so far as they are directed against the university itself, are perhaps against the inability of those in the arts and humanities to control the application of the discoveries of their colleagues in the sciences.

If universities could attain the objectives assigned to them they would, indeed, change their societies profoundly. They would become the most powerful institutions for change and innovation. As they work at present, however, the only innovations of which they seem capable appear to bring as many disadvantages as advantages. Until they can prove themselves capable of more constructive outcomes, or of controlling the competitiveness and destructiveness that go with these innovations, they have to be prevented from realizing their aims. And until all the other power-hungry groups of society are prepared to yield priority as change agents to the universities, they will be prevented. Muddling university constitutions, confusing their organizations and making them the targets for attack, are among the instruments used by society to ensure their continuing failure. The disorganization is powerfully motivated.

The report of the Indian Education Commission reads (page 325):

'Unfortunately, the problems special to university governance have not received adequate attention. . . . A resolute effort needs to be made to evolve policies, techniques and practices, and a machinery for decision-making needed for a forward looking and dynamic academic organization.'

I have argued that more than a machinery for decision-making is required. Without a change of culture, no new organization is likely to work satisfactorily. Nevertheless, as the Commission also states:

'What is worse, rules, procedures and techniques, once adopted, tend to be continued indefinitely in their original form, even when changed conditions and circumstances have made them obsolete or incompatible with the real needs and practices of institutions. Such rigidity seriously retards progress and development.'

In other words, the rigidity of the procedures and techniques becomes a part of the culture which reinforces the resistance to innovation and change. The difficulty is to find a conceptual framework that will permit analysis of the problems of university governance. Detailed research into different aspects of university objectives, protests against specific practices, are unlikely to produce other than conflicting results unless the complexity of the structure and culture of the whole can be comprehended. At the same time, there can be little argument that university objectives, however defined, require the performance of a number of interdependent tasks. Education is by definition a change process. If it is not innovative it becomes sterile.

For the purposes of the next two chapters I shall treat a university as though it had two major sub-systems: one for the discovery of knowledge – research; the other for the dissemination of knowledge – teaching. Each of these sub-systems has a characteristic throughput that differentiates it from the other; and each of the sub-systems has sub-sub-systems, again, each with a throughput that differentiates it from other sub-sub-systems. Thus the teaching sub-system, whose characteristic throughput consists of students, has sub-sub-systems whose characteristic throughputs are students reading different subjects at different stages, and other sub-sub-systems concerned with providing opportunities for growth and maturation. In the same way, the research sub-system has sub-sub-systems whose throughput depends on the kind of research being carried out, whether the objective is to discover knowledge in general or to seek solutions to specific problems.

Nowhere, so far as I can discover, has any explicit order of priority been assigned to the tasks of these sub-systems or sub-sub-systems. In building organizational models, therefore, I shall first of all consider the various tasks related to different throughputs as independent of each other, as capable of performance in isolation. I shall leave to Chapter 6 the integration of the models into one system for undergraduate education. Similarly, in Chapter 7 I shall treat post-

UNIVERSITY OBJECTIVES

graduate education as independent of undergraduate education and leave to Chapter 8 the integration of undergraduate and postgraduate education into a model organization for a university. This method has the advantage that it allows the building of organizational models, treating each sub-system task as the primary task to which all others are subservient. It has the disadvantage that each task, taken in isolation, appears limited in definition and restricted in performance. I believe, however, that prior consideration of the independent values of the tasks may help to reduce confusion when it becomes necessary to consider the control of their interdependence.

CHAPTER 4

Organizational Model for Task Performance: Research

Under research, I include the discovery of new knowledge, the extension of existing knowledge, and application when application itself requires investigation. I do not subscribe to the view that it is possible to draw viable or even useful boundaries between basic and applied research or even between research and development. Most of the arguments about such differences appear to have been bedevilled by attempts to prove that the one or the other has higher status or is of more value in human affairs. I find the distinctions arbitrary, and, particularly in the social sciences, positively disruptive as determinants of research organization and control. Different kinds of research require different organizations, the exercise of different kinds of authority, and hence different kinds of management.

THE CLASSIFICATION OF RESEARCH WORK

In a later chapter, when I come to consider constraints on task performance, I shall speculate on the reasons for the trend towards the differentiation of 'pure' and 'applied' science; in this chapter, and as a preliminary to the examination of research organization, I wish to put forward a matrix into which I think all research work can be fitted. The matrix is three-dimensional:

(a) Question formulation: the precision with which questions can be asked, and hence the ease or difficulty with which answers can be found. The dimension extends from the precise to the vague; from the consideration of simple to the consideration of multiple variables.

(b) Techniques of investigation: the dimension extends from the known, well-tried, and authenticated techniques to the unknown. At the latter end of the continuum the first problem is to formulate a question, the second to discover how an investigation can be made.

(c) Control of source of data: the dimension extends from the situation in which the research worker can have such complete control over the source of his data that he can isolate his variables, investigate in any way he wishes, and publish his findings, to the situation in which he has such incomplete control that it is frequently doubtful whether the source does not control the investigation. This type of investigation has to deal with multiple variables, of which few are usually measurable and many are unknown, and publication in any detailed form invariably depends on getting permission from the source of the data.

An example of research work at or close to the zero point of all dimensions would be an investigation into the properties of an inorganic compound. The questions can be precise; the techniques of investigation are well established; the source of data can be completely controlled in the laboratory, and there are no barriers to the publication of results. At the other end of all dimensions would be an investigation into a community riot. The questions that can be asked are generally vague; such techniques as have been invented have not so far yielded very useful results; and control of the source of data, or controlled experiment, is usually impossible. Publication of such findings as can be obtained may lead to legal action or even to further violence.

At one end of the continua, the 'basic science' end, a junior research worker can be instructed in technique, his source of data can be given to him, and his work can be supervised as closely as is necessary. At the other, the worker often has to formulate his own questions, develop appropriate techniques, and make his own relationships with the source of his data. The only valid control is 'professional'. By 'professional' control I mean that the research worker has to subscribe to an explicit code of behaviour that prohibits him from taking any action, or making any intervention, that might harm the source of his data. Action or intervention for the sake of research, without consideration of its effect on the respondent, is inexcusable. The research worker has to be trusted. This is a condition that presents particular difficulties in medical and social research. Patients and respondents are not always willing to trust their illnesses, or their behaviour, to the scrutiny of untried, inexperienced, young research workers. The poor have perhaps been over-used by medicine as the major source of data; and social science professors have perhaps played too many games with their students for the results always to be accepted as meaningful in real life.

My own prejudice is clear: it does not seem to me that investigations are more or less 'pure', or 'basic', because they are at different points on the three dimensions. Variables may be more or less numerous, known, complex, and interdependent; results may be more or less measurable; and experiments more or less controllable. But I take an investigation to be scientific if the method is scientific – that is, if the thinking is ruthless and a clear distinction is made between fact, hypothesis, and speculation. That a hypothesis is not rigorously testable, or an experiment not controllable or exactly replicable, means only that the necessary techniques have not yet been discovered. I certainly feel that the premature measurement of the irrelevant is no way of making an 'applied' or 'clinical' science 'purer' or more 'basic'.

I propose to take up some of the implications of this way of looking at research when I come to consider the problems of the university status system; here, I wish to discuss research work according to whether the throughput can be identified as:

(a) scientists – the throughput on which most university research organization is modelled; or

(b) problems – the dominant throughput of most government or industrial research and, in recent years, of more and more university research.

SCIENTISTS AS THE THROUGHPUT

Strictly speaking, the intake into a system designed for the discovery of knowledge is a question; the conversion processes are the thinking, searching, and experimentation prompted by the question; and the output is the answer. The point is that if only the right questions could be asked, answers would be comparatively easy to find. For the discovery of new knowledge – and I accept that much so-called 'new knowledge' is either the rediscovery of what has been known before, or the extension or reformulation of existing knowledge – the intake could therefore be defined as curiosity; the activities of the conversion process could be defined as the probings and questioning that curiosity provokes; the output as an answerable question. In practice, this means the intake is man; the conversion processes are what he thinks, feels, and does; the output is what he communicates.

The organization of research in universities has usually been based on such a process, or something very like it. Creative individuals have been appointed; they have worked on their own, or they have built groups round themselves, established laboratories, retreats, or other forms of protection from interference, and worked therein. Their outputs have attracted resources to maintain and expand the institutions they have built. Autonomy is taken for granted; control of, and commitment to, the task are intrinsic. Organization becomes in reality only an instrument of task performance, to be modified, changed, or discarded without regard to precedent, established roles, or role relationships. Task and sentient systems coincide, that is, total commitment to the task and to the task group is expected. Dissidents have to leave. This is the classical egalitarian and informal structure of sophisticated research groups.

Unfortunately, perhaps, the model has been applied, or has vociferously been claimed to apply, not only to those who are genuinely creative, but to most research work and research workers, and to most research institutions irrespective of their size and purpose. In universities, 'academic freedom' has become a banner that is in danger of degenerating into a cliché. I do not doubt that universities should provide appropriate conditions for creative workers; but I question the extension of the freedom and autonomy to all who claim to do research. Real ability should always be endowed, but if fear of making judgements about ability leads to the subsidization of mediocrity, then, in the long run, sponsors are likely to revolt. Even private donors in an affluent society usually expect a minimum pay-off for their sponsorship – generally prestige. A nation, a state, or community that provides resources to support university research and research workers eventually demands the kind of output it requires. I turn next, therefore, to the organization of a research institution of which the intakes are problems and the outputs are solutions.

PROBLEM-CENTRED RESEARCH

In this section I am considering research units or groups which, for the most part, will be judged by their capacity to find solutions to problems of short- or long-term concern to their sponsors. I accept that many problems will be self-generated, that is, they will be formulated by the research workers within the research unit. I also accept that genuinely innovative and creative answers may be found to questions that have not been asked, as well as to those that have. The dominant import-conversion-export process of such a unit, however, imports problems, either presented by the sponsors, or defined by the research workers in the interests of the sponsors; the conversion processes are the collection and analysis of data and the conduct of experiments; and the outputs are solutions in the form of published findings or working models. Or, because solutions are seldom complete, outputs may be the problems reformulated in such a way that further work can be done.

The resources required for task performance are research workers and their equipment. The basic operating system is therefore a 'project' – workers and equipment – assembled to solve a problem. Once it is solved, or other problems are formulated, the project has served its purpose and is disbanded. The operating systems are therefore essentially temporary.

Controls are required at the boundaries of the unit to ensure that appropriate problems are imported (or generated), that adequate resources are available, and that outputs at least give sufficient satisfaction to sponsors to ensure continuing support. Internally, controls are required to see that resources are properly used and that appropriate priorities are assigned to projects. Research workers who wish to exercise 'freedom', and to take off on a line of their own, can do so only if the line they wish to take is relevant to sponsors' needs. Alternatively, they have to find different sources of support and leave the unit.

The management controls described are not easy, particularly when a project team has been successful in inventing a new technique of investigation or in solving some problem. The team is only too apt to become imprisoned by its own success. Unwittingly, its members search for new areas to which they can apply their technique, or for new problems to enable them to preserve their identity. Research-unit management has to provide two basic control and service functions: adequate sentient systems for research workers who are constantly being put together and disbanded, and control of the use of scarce and expensive equipment. A successful project team invariably develops sentience; its members become committed to working together. Such identification can be a powerful reinforcement to task performance: admirable and desirable while the project on which the team is working is consistent with the objectives of the unit; disruptive when the project, however intrinsically valuable, is irrelevant to unit objectives and uses up unit resources. Sentient systems, differentiated from operating systems, are essential to provide alternative identification and to maintain institutional rather than project commitment. Discipline-based departments, or other groups to which members are prepared to commit themselves, can provide a management control over the adequacy of resources and their use. They can also provide a base for project workers, where they can discuss their problems and enrich their specific skills. But departments or groups of this kind are control and service functions in the managing system of a problem-centred research unit, not operating systems.

In the same way, expensive resources and equipment in short supply are often required by more than one project, for example, space, laboratories, computers, money. Members of a successful project team are only too ready to claim such resources as their own as a means of reinforcing their sentience and of avoiding their disbandment. Controls that keep track of the use and maintenance of equipment are therefore also required.

A model organization of a research unit of this kind – for convenience called a problem-centred research institute – is shown in *Figure 6*. In practice, institute management will usually control directly the import and export systems, accepting problems and assigning them to project teams, checking findings before they are published, and handing over pilot models as operating organizations. An important point about such a model is that operating systems and their management – the essential systems by which the institute's

FIGURE 6 *Model organization for a problem-centred and/or multidisciplinary research institute*

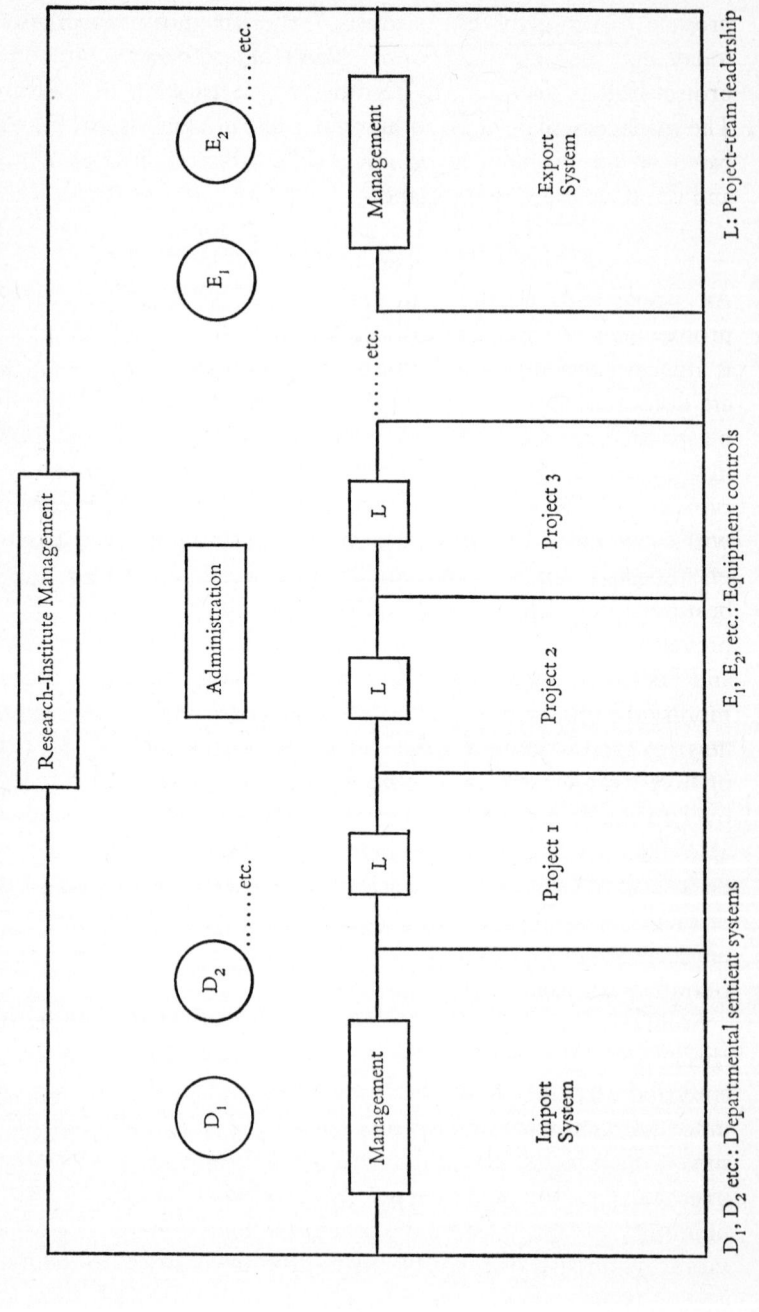

D_1, D_2 etc.: Departmental sentient systems E_1, E_2, etc.: Equipment controls L: Project-team leadership

primary task is performed – are impermanent. As such, they do not provide career paths for scientists. True, the project assistants of today may become the project leaders of tomorrow; but today's project leaders may have to become project assistants in the future. The management decision about who leads, and who assists, has to be based on the problem to be solved, the skills required to solve it, and the time it is likely to take.

RESEARCH-PROGRAMME MANAGEMENT

An important variation on the project-type organization of a problem-centred research institute occurs when a series of projects is amalgamated into a programme. To the extent that the projects are distinguishable from each other they require separate leadership, but to the extent that they are alike, or are within the same field of investigation, they require common leadership at a higher order. A typical example would be an attempt to discover and experiment with a new kind of community service. A community need is known or suspected: for example, for legal advice or for a new kind of health service. The objectives are: to investigate the need and its prevalence, how it affects the lives of the members of the community, and how to meet it; to set up a pilot model to meet the need; to modify the model in the light of experience; to evaluate its effectiveness; to train workers for the service; to learn from the experience of investigation, setting up, and evaluation; and, finally, to hand it over to the community as a going enterprise. The number of variables the original team has to take into account is considerable, and, because the experiment is by definition breaking new ground, many of them are likely to be unknown. Even the skills required may be uncertain, and the programme team will have to be able to acquire resources as it finds them necessary.

Substantial autonomy is essential. Administrative procedures, checks and balances, that are appropriate to established large-scale enterprises cannot be allowed to slow down, or inhibit, necessary innovation and experiment. Any form of organization with which such a team starts out may have to be modified, if not drastically overhauled, at frequent intervals. As experience is gained, new lines of inquiry and new possibilities for experiment open up. The organization required is one that has maximum flexibility consistent with the necessary minimum controls over the use of resources. In effect, a single programme usually starts as a quasi-autonomous project, which, if it is successful, quickly develops sub-projects. These, in their turn, become quasi-autonomous projects within the programme. The more successful of these then develop into programmes in their own right.

At this stage, problems of organization tend to become acute. Ideally, such programmes require the same facilities and level of autonomy as the original programme of which they were a part. In practice, I believe that such second and subsequent generations of programmes are more likely to thrive if, like other organic systems, they are given their independence when they come of age. They may still belong to the original family, but, like members of other families, they are expected, so far as resources are concerned, to justify their own existence. Organizationally, the original programme becomes a federation of quasi-autonomous states, some of whose members eventually may, as their programmes develop, secede from their original parent federation, either to join up with other federations or to form new federations of their own. The model organization is still of a basic project type, but with task and sentient systems coinciding at the level of the programme. The number of control and service functions is small and their interrelations are simple. Nor are such programme teams likely to need complex management roles. They do, however, require leadership that not only allows but encourages movement of constituent parts towards independence; leadership, in effect, that encourages and fosters its own rivals.

SPECIALIZATION

I have differentiated specialization from research, not because I believe it is not dependent on a throughput of scientists, or because it cannot be problem-centred, but because of the potential conflict between discipline-based and multidisciplinary research. Pushing forward the frontiers of knowledge is biased in favour of specialization – pushing in depth within a narrow field. This, after all, is how specializations are developed. Organizationally, therefore, in spite of what is written above, much research work, and particularly university research work, is likely to be discipline-based and to be carried on in discipline-based departments, or at least to have a starting-point in a particular discipline. As the knowledge grows deeper, and the level of abstraction rises, disciplines are of course likely to lose the special characteristics that differentiate them from one another. But that means only a redrawing of departmental boundaries – a process that could be evolutionary rather than revolutionary, were it not for the vested interests that defend historical boundaries with such vehemence.

The actual organization of departmental research can be 'scientist-based' or 'problem-centred'. In discipline-based research, however, research management is essentially departmental management also, and as such is likely to be responsible for other departmental activities such as teaching. In this sense the department, in contrast to the department in a problem-centred research institute, is the operating system. The important point is that as soon as the research work requires access to a source of data that cannot be controlled, or moves across the boundaries of other discipline-based departments, a different kind of organization is required – in effect, the temporary and transitional project type of organization.

The point was perhaps less important when universities were not under such pressure from society to address themselves to the solution of contemporary social problems, and when knowledge was discovered at a rate at which it was comprehensible and hence controllable. Today, the explosion of knowledge has led, on the one hand, to a proliferation of specializations, and, on the other, to increasing difficulty in comprehending their interdependence. Even if the conflicts and misunderstandings between different disciplines in the same broad scientific areas are ignored, it often seems to the outsider that the natural, biological, and human sciences are each pursuing such different and divergent courses that their application to human affairs can lead only to contradictory results. The invention of new pesticides that increase our food supply bids fair to ruin the environment on which we depend for it; the discoveries in biology that have so greatly advanced our understanding of the origins of life itself seem only too likely to provide us with more efficient means of destroying it; and the humanities, which have previously shaped our value systems, appear often to have been left stranded in an increasingly sterile textual exegesis of the classics.

The conflicts between the natural, biological, and human sciences are exacerbated when the role and activities of the postgraduate research student are considered. This subject more properly belongs to Chapter 7, when I shall be looking at the appropriate organization to deal with the throughput of postgraduate education. Here I wish to note only the confusion of goals that so often exists among postgraduate students: to carry out original research work; to learn research techniques that will enable them to become research workers; or to earn higher degrees that will give them higher status and enable them to obtain better jobs irrespective of the relationship between their research and the job they take. I accept that all three are important, but I believe that university postgraduate departments are frequently in some difficulty about their primary task: to discover new knowledge, to solve problems, to train research workers, or to award degrees. Without research work, research workers cannot be trained. But it has to be admitted that much research work is hampered by a clutter of postgraduate students wanting higher degrees and needing supervision.

The research student who is chosen by the creative research worker, and who finds he can hold his own in such company, is indeed privileged. He may or may not be well instructed in research techniques, and he may or may not make a significant contribution to knowledge, but he has in front of him a model of creative endeavour with which he can identify, and which can stimulate and excite him. But unless the student is exceptional, such a climate of research can be too rarefied. I suspect that the majority of doctoral candidates fare better, and are better trained, in laboratories and other kinds of research institution in which research techniques can be taught, in which the research is directed towards clearly formulated problems, and in which the finding of research problems for postgraduate students to work on is not a major distraction.

In other words, my hypothesis is that the normal postgraduate student is likely to do better if his research work is in a discipline-based department. At least, this will be so if his primary goal is to get a doctorate.

AN ORGANIZATIONAL MODEL FOR UNIVERSITY-BASED RESEARCH

If I can assume that the majority of postgraduate students will be located in discipline-based departments, and that those attached to creative research workers or to problem-centred research institutes will be so attached only because they are needed for the research tasks, there are still three kinds of research enterprise, representing three different throughputs, that have to be accommodated in university-based research: discipline-based departments, research institutes (working on a class of similar problems or in a field that requires multidisciplinary research), and research groups headed by tycoons (to borrow a word from industry to represent what is essentially the one-man business). The operating systems are shown in *Figure 7*.

For the sake of completeness, I have put all the operating systems within a boundary controlled by 'Research Management'. If research were the only task of a university, some such control on behalf of the university would be required. The major decision-making process of such a function is investment; or, to put it more crudely, deciding on whom to bet, how much, and for how long. Whether such a differentiated management function is required in the multiple-task system of a university I propose to discuss in Chapters 6, 7, and 8 when I have to take up task interdependence. But whether the differentiated function is required or not, the investment decision-making function certainly is.

A major management control problem with such an array of enterprises is the location of sentient groups. When I discussed problem-centred research, I suggested that discipline-based departments could provide appropriate sentient groups for members of project teams. They are shown as second-order control and service functions in the managing system of Research Institute 1 in *Figure 7*. But, in the model organization, discipline-based departments also appear as operating systems in their own right for specialized research. Consequently, if these departments are used by members of the project teams of the research institutes as their sentient groups, the members are committing themselves to, and identifying with, groups outside the boundaries of their own 'institutes'. The

FIGURE 7 *The operating systems of university-based research*

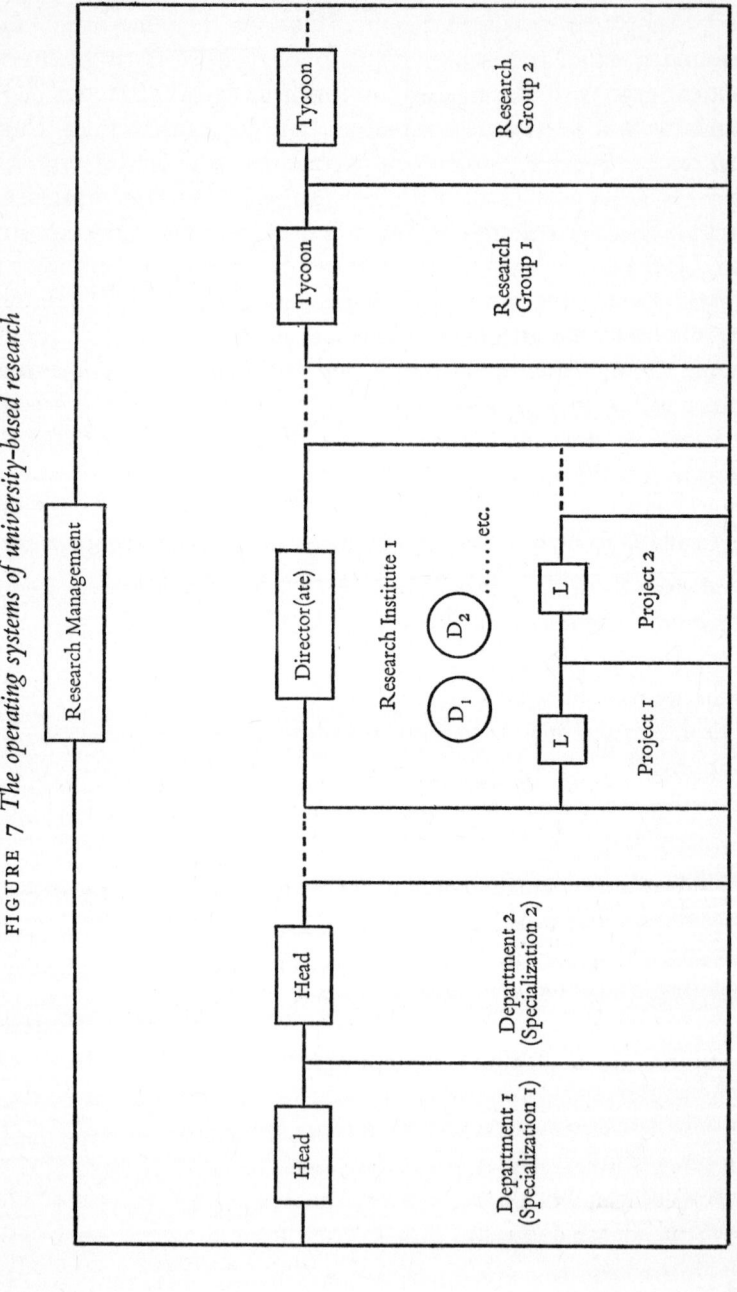

D₁, D₂, etc.: Departments as sentient groups L: Project leader

task-system boundaries of the problem-centred research institutes are very likely to be weakened thereby. But if, on the other hand, each research institute tries to set up its own separate discipline-based sentient groups, it is, perhaps, too much to expect that very high standards will be endlessly repeated. It is no great wonder, then, that discipline-based departments can become so powerful, and that they should appear as major threats to research groups engaged in multidisciplinary research of the kind in which little or no control can be maintained over the source of data; or that professional schools should have to insist on mantaining their own 'basic' research lest university departments (which are invariably discipline-based) should capture their best scientists. Such insistence will be unavoidable, until the university as a whole is prepared to change its concepts of scientific purity, and hence its status hierarchy.

So far as most universities are concerned, all three kinds of research enterprise already exist. From the organizational point of view, all that appears to be required in practice is more formal recognition:

(a) that the three types of enterprise are different, and hence require different kinds of management;

(b) that the setting up of quasi-autonomous research institutes is the appropriate strategy for moving into the investigation of social problems and any other problems that require a multidisciplinary approach;

(c) that traditional departments have to become temporary and transitional task systems: that is, they have to be prepared to divide as specialization increases and to reintegrate into different kinds of departments as the development of theory demonstrates the need for different kinds of combination.

Such organizational differentiations would mean that 'basic science' departments could not remain the only possible high-status sentient groups to which members of the faculty would belong. But I doubt whether the problems that exist are wholly organizational. I am only too aware that organizational change by itself may be useless; there is seldom any purely organizational solution to motivated disorganization while the motives that caused the disorganization remain unchanged. This and similar practical problems I propose to take up in later chapters.

A final note on university organization concerns the many members of faculty who receive financial support for their research work as individuals in their own right. They are not directly supported by the university, and hence cannot be controlled in quite the same way as those who are directly financed by it. In effect: pushed, they can take their grants elsewhere. Such research workers are among those I have called 'tycoons'. The only real investment the university makes in their case is in giving them facilities to work; the pay-off lies in the prestige that accrues to the university from their success. Organizationally, this is an investment decision just like any other; the same calculation is required: What return is likely for the investment made? With regard to such a tycoon, the investment considerations are: the amount of space his unit requires against the competition from other departments and institutes; the probable indirect cost that will result to other systems from the inclusion of such a unit; and whether the creation of the unit will be regarded with favour or disfavour by other workers. Decisions on these matters are difficult, often extremely so, and negotiations between tycoon and university frequently appear to smack of mutual blackmail; but these are not, I believe, good reasons for distorting organization.

Any research process has an in-built tendency towards the formation of a relatively closed system, in which self-generated intakes crowd out intakes from the external environment, and answers to self-generated questions are, in their turn, reimported into the system as new questions. Research institutions have, therefore, a natural tendency to become divorced from their environments, and their boundaries tend to become increasingly impermeable. Apart from the extent to which the support of an institution may depend on its being maintained as an open system, it is also likely that the institution's capacity for creative problem-solving will decline without the feedback that accompanies transactions with relevant parts of its environment. One relevant environment for university-based research work is, of course, work in similar fields in other universities; the danger is that, while a particular university department or research institute may not itself become a closed system, academic research in the same or similar fields may. The result is a self-perpetuating closed system, which, because of the exchanges with other universities, provides a myth of openness.

CHAPTER 5

Organizational Model for Task Performance: Education

An institution whose primary task is education has students as intakes; teaching as the activities of the conversion systems; and those who have learned, or have failed to learn, as outputs. The measure of the productivity of the system is the difference between intakes and outputs, usually symbolized by the award, or non-award, of a degree or diploma. The resources required for task performance are teachers and the appropriate buildings and equipment. The process is shown in *Figure 8*.

FIGURE 8 *Dominant import-conversion-export process for the primary task of education*

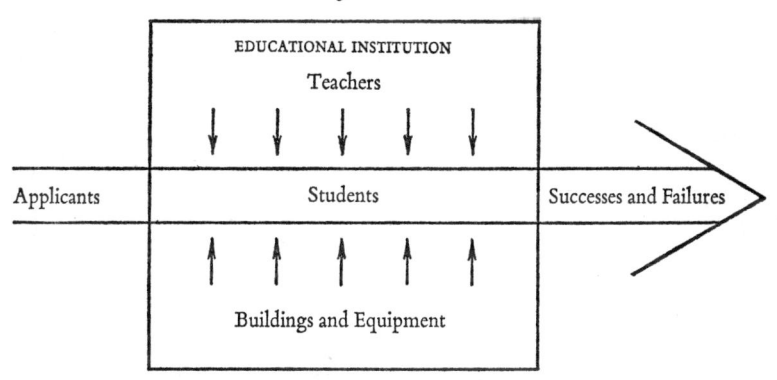

```
              EDUCATIONAL INSTITUTION
                    Teachers
                ↓  ↓  ↓  ↓  ↓
Applicants │     Students        │  Successes and Failures  ⟩
                ↑  ↑  ↑  ↑  ↑
              Buildings and Equipment
```

In 'education' I include the whole range of teaching from direct instruction in what is known to discussion of what is only partly or incompletely known. (The brilliant student may indeed outreach his teachers.) I also include what might best be described as intellectual training or the integration of knowledge, and the provision of opportunities for growth and maturation. These processes do not involve teaching in the conventional sense. The task of the faculty is

41

to provide means whereby the student can learn for himself, through behaviour as well as through verbal and written communications.

The obvious boundary controls are at entry to, and exit from, the educational institution, between various courses within the same institution, and between the various stages of each course. The less obvious are between different teachers teaching the same subject and between different subjects being taught in the same course.

THE OPERATING SYSTEMS OF EDUCATION

The essential task system for education contains teacher and students. How well the task is performed will depend not only on the knowledge of the teacher and his capacity to teach, and on the intelligence of the students and their willingness to learn, but also on the relationships established between teacher and students. It seems clear, therefore, that the task will be performed most successfully (given competent and willing participants) if the teacher can choose whom he will teach, and the students by whom they will be taught. Notwithstanding such choices, the teacher has the responsibility, and should have the authority, to decide what to teach and how to teach it. His is the assigned leadership role.

So much for the ideal. Problems of management control arise, however, when more than one subject is taught in a course, and when more than one teacher teaches a subject. If each teacher has the right to determine what is taught and how, students (for whom the institution exists) are likely to be confused by inconsistencies of knowledge, method, and teaching capacity among their teachers – even apart from the confusion that arises from their own different learning capabilities. From the student's point of view, the different subjects of a course should have some coherence, some relationship to each other. To maintain internal consistency for subjects and coherence for courses, two levels of control are necessary: for convenience described as 'departmental' for subjects, and 'faculty' for courses. But the very existence of these differentiated controls means that the individual teacher's right to admit and not to admit students, and to choose what and how to teach them, must be subordinated, at least to some extent, to faculty control of course boundaries and to departmental control of subject boundaries.

An organizational model for a very simple educational institu-

FIGURE 9 *Organizational model for a one-course (one-faculty) five-subject educational institution*

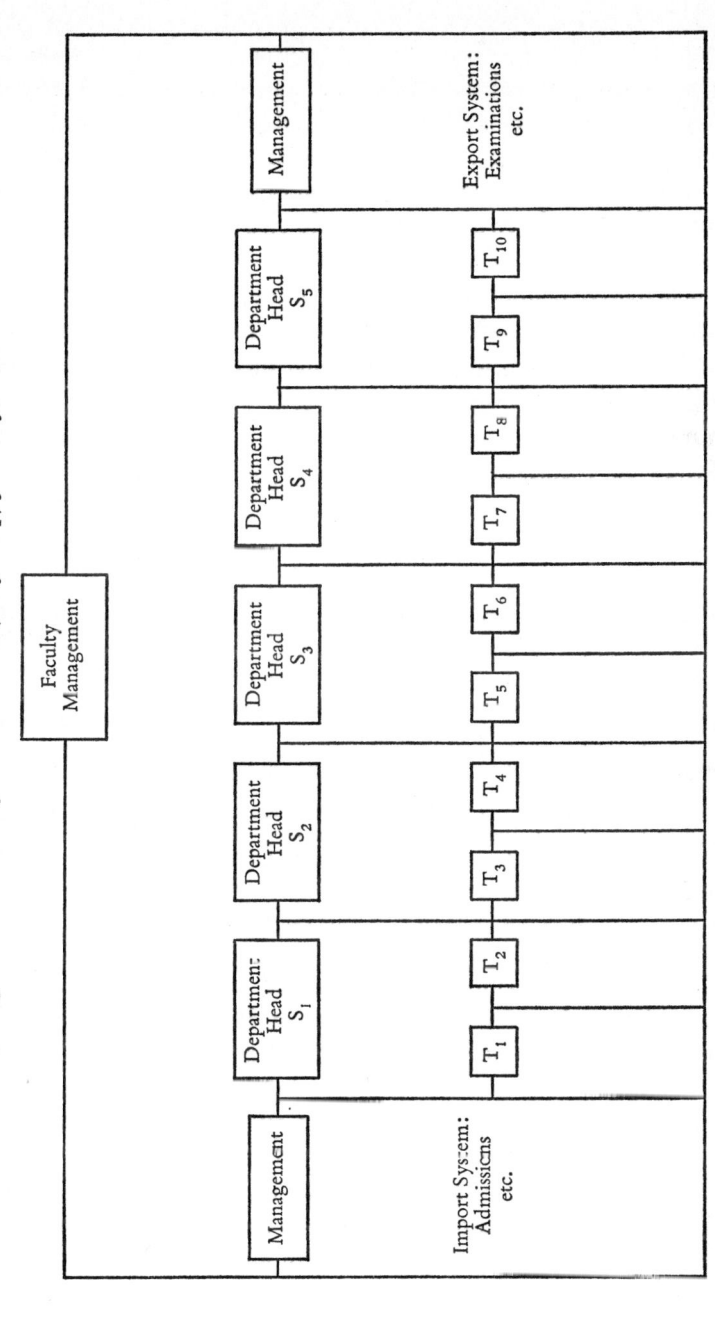

S_1, S_2, etc.: Subjects T_1, T_2, etc.: Teachers

tion, teaching only one course in one stage, with five different subjects and two teachers for each subject, is shown in *Figure 9*, in which subjects are labelled $S_1, S_2, \ldots$, and teachers $T_1, T_2 \ldots$

As soon as I move to an institution offering more than one course in more than one stage, far more boundary controls are required. To illustrate this I imagine what is still a very simple educational institution, offering only two courses in only two stages (for example, first and second years). Each course consists of two subjects running concurrently, neither of which is common to both courses. The throughput is shown in *Figure 10*. The corresponding organizational model is shown in *Figure 11*, in which there are two faculties each with two departments, corresponding to the two courses and four subjects.

FIGURE 10 *Throughput of two courses, each with two subjects and two stages*

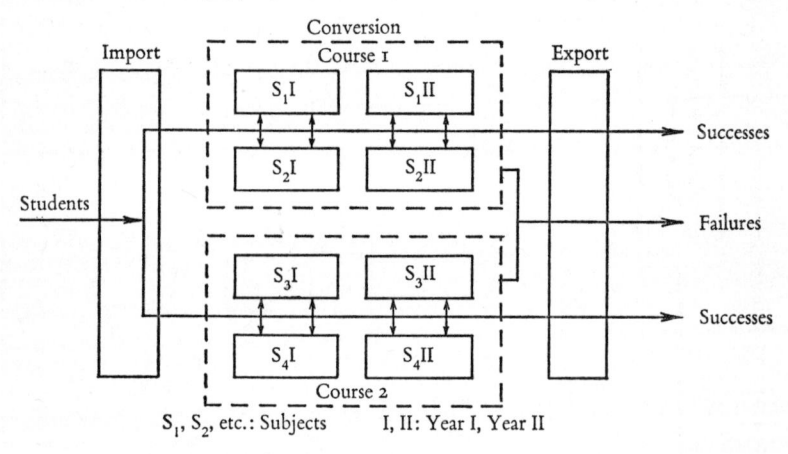

S_1, S_2, etc.: Subjects   I, II: Year I, Year II

The additional controls now required are at entry to and exit from the total institution as well as at faculty and departmental levels, and between stages within departments. If management of the total institution is to control its boundaries, it must control the standards of entry of students and the qualifications that determine graduates or failures. Faculties cannot therefore have the sole right to include or exclude students. If they did, then students could be admitted to the institution but find no course to attend. If, on the other hand, management of the institution delegates the authority to include or to exclude to faculties, then students may have to try

FIGURE 1.1 *Outline organization of a simple educational institution*

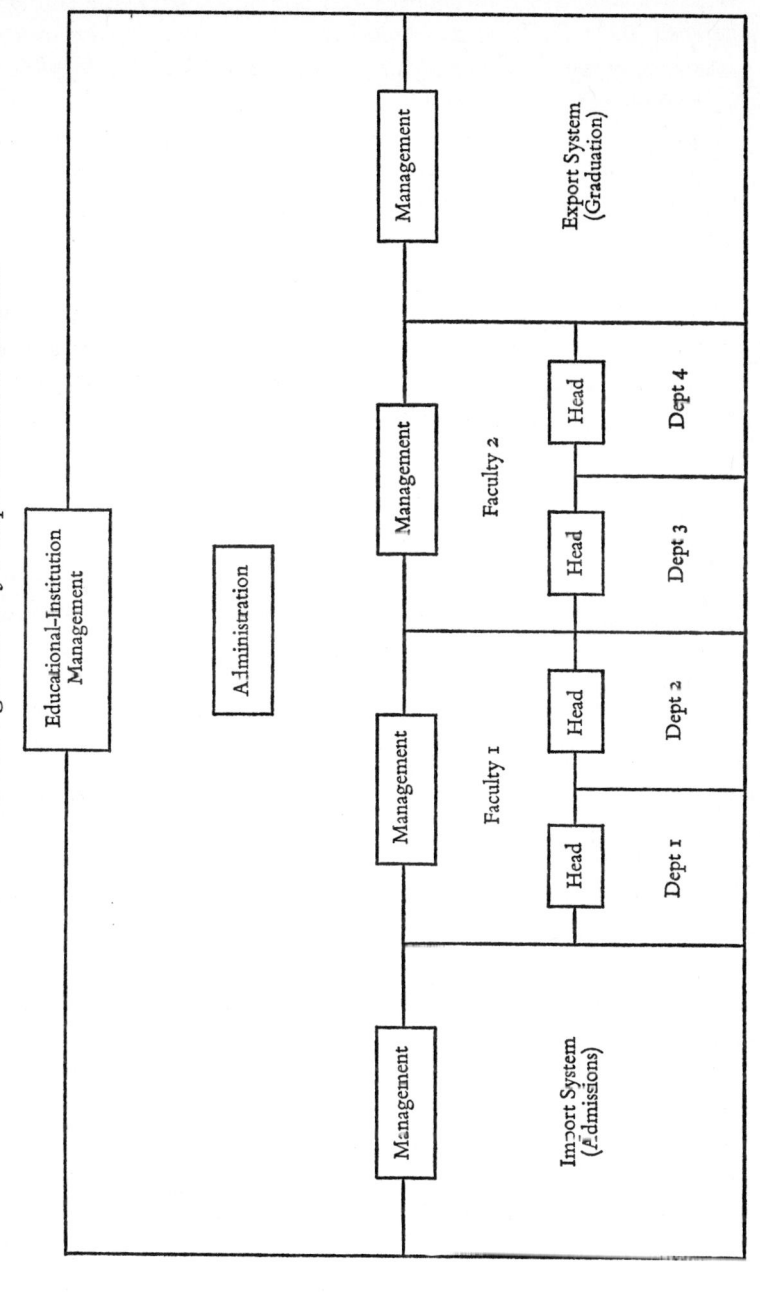

to enter all courses to make as sure as possible of getting into the institution at all. Institutional management, unless it is to abdicate control of transactions across its most important boundary, will have to impose control mechanisms in order to maintain some measure of consistency between the standards of inclusion, exclusion, and graduation of the different faculties.

In practice, it is usual for the management of the import and export systems to be undertaken jointly by institutional and faculty managements; and for faculty management to use departmental heads and staff to determine standards of entry into, and exit from, courses. I do not wish to suggest that the practice is necessarily wrong; but I do suggest that lack of organizational clarity about who is doing what, and on whose behalf, is one of the causes contributing to student dissatisfaction about standards of admission and graduation. Authority and responsibility appear to be claimed and disclaimed with impartial confusion by members of faculties and by institutional management.

So far, I have considered very simple institutions, but it is of course probable that in most higher educational institutions some subjects will be common to more than one course. Where this occurs it is necessary to coordinate and control the teaching of the same subject in different courses. At this stage a decision has to be made about the relative authority of those responsible for courses – heads of faculties – and those responsible for subjects – heads of departments. Organizationally, the decision should be based on the needs of the throughput – the students. What the student learns has to be internalized and integrated into his previous knowledge and future aspirations. This is clearly more likely if he takes an integrated course and not just a collection of subjects. The major operating systems should therefore be faculties and not departments (as shown in *Figure 11*). Departments that teach in only one faculty are thus subordinate to faculty management; but those that are responsible for the same subject in more than one faculty have to be operating systems in their own right. One faculty can obviously make a contract to have its students attend another faculty's course. And, as will be seen when I come to consider the overall model for a university, I accept such contracts as practical compromises. But I also have to insist that such compromises require ruthless boundary

MODEL FOR TASK PERFORMANCE: EDUCATION

definition to ensure that both faculty and students are aware of the nature of the contract and particularly of its limitations.

The throughput process of a two-course, five-subject, educational institution, with one subject common to both courses, is shown in *Figure 12*, and the corresponding organization is presented in *Figure 13*. In *Figure 13* it will be seen that the head of the department

FIGURE 12 *Throughput of two courses, each with three subjects, one of which is common to both courses*

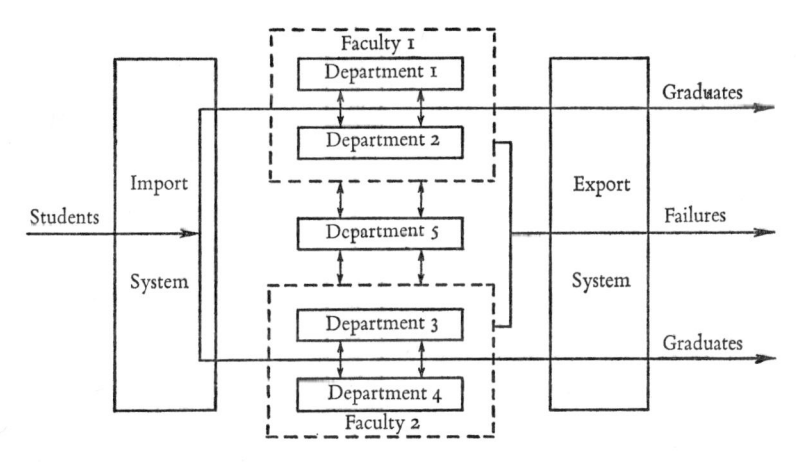

teaching subject 5 (common to both courses) has become head of a separate and differentiated operating system. The appropriate implication is that, if the department offering subject 5 does not, in the eyes of faculty managements 1 and 2, function effectively, they have either to demand its replacement or to set up separate departments in their own faculties to teach subject 5. Such departments, like the departments responsible for subjects 1, 2, 3, and 4, would then become subordinate to the respective faculty managements, and department 5 would be deprived of students.

THE INTEGRATION OF LEARNING

The explosion of knowledge of recent years, particularly in the sciences, has led to more and more differentiation between the different branches of knowledge, and hence to the development of

FIGURE 13 *Model organization for an educational institution with throughput of Figure 12*

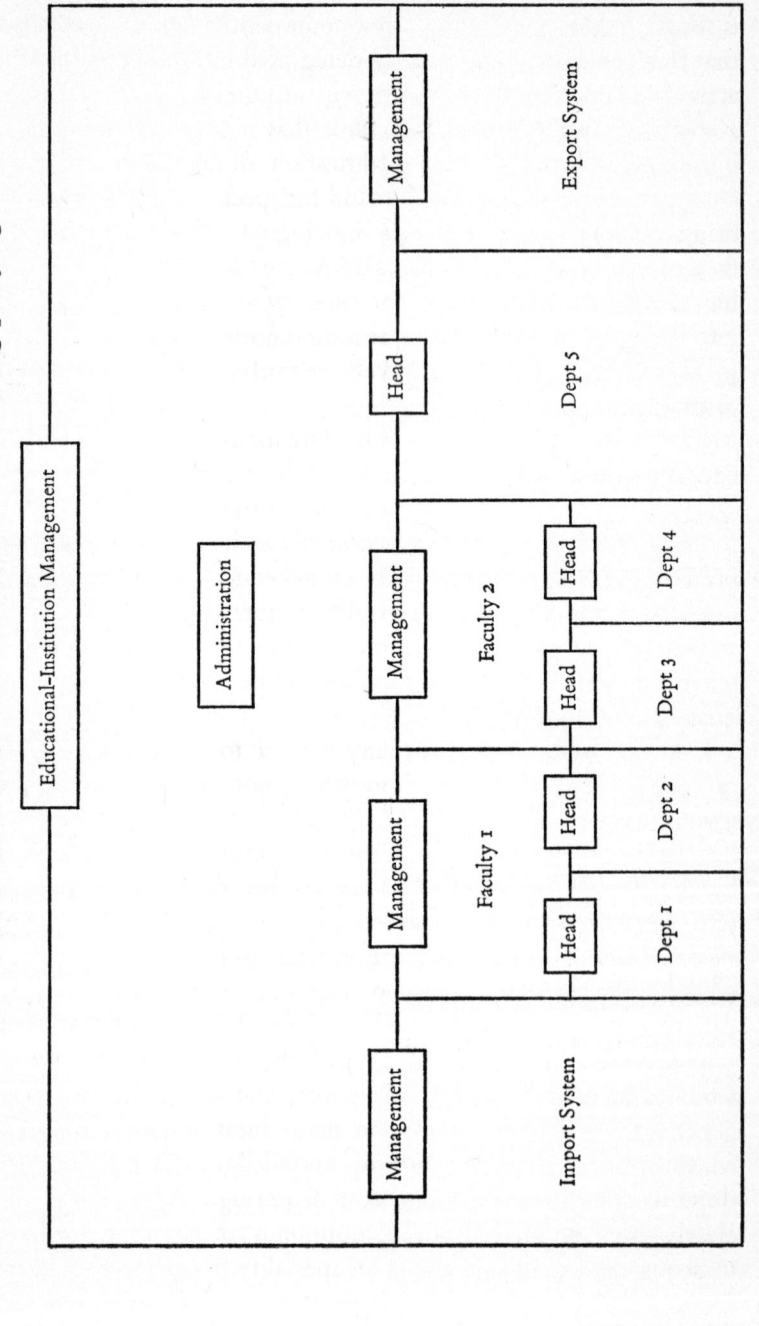

more and more specialization. To know something of many branches is usually a bar to knowing any one in depth. One consequence is that the 'generalist' is frequently denigrated by the specialist, if not actively despised. And the student who acquires a general, rather than a specialist, qualification often finds that it is of less value in the outside world than is the qualification of his more specialized colleague. Nevertheless, the demand for specialist qualifications that bring brighter career prospects and higher status frequently conflicts, not only with the student's own desire for a broader education, but also with society's need for those who can bring some order into the chaos caused by the increasing fragmentation of knowledge. In the West, until comparatively recently, a classical education, primarily the study of the literature, philosophy, and history of dead Mediterranean civilizations, was held by many to provide a rounded education. In other parts of the world the study of the accumulated wisdom of their own past was the corresponding field. More recently, the 'liberal arts', not necessarily including the classics, have been believed to provide not only a good education but an admirable intellectual training. And now today, numeracy, as well as literacy, is believed essential; a man must comprehend the language of science, as well as that of the arts, before he can be considered adequately educated.

I do not pretend to have any answer to this dilemma, but I can suggest that good education should not reinforce the contradiction between generalist and specialist. It has to be admitted, however, that attempts so far to provide a more rounded education – by the introduction of general courses before, or general subjects into, specialized training – have not met with more than a qualified success. Indeed, either specialization tends to be required earlier and earlier in the educational process, as in the United Kingdom, or the educational process is abnormally prolonged into maturity, as in the United States. Among university staff, the same forces and pressures tend to fissiparity between disciplines, and to denigration of the generalist. I make the assumption that education, in the true sense, consists not so much in acquiring knowledge, either about everything or about just one thing, as in acquiring the capacity to think clearly about anything. If this assumption is correct, then, in addition to acquiring knowledge about his speciality, a student should have adequate opportunities to think for himself, to have his ideas questioned, and to question the ideas of others. If he is to acquire the capacity to think, he needs practice, and probably some guidance while he practises.

To give such practice requires a different kind of teacher role. The basic task system consists of a 'supervisor' with a student or a group of students. The student prepares work, discusses it, hears it criticized, and responds to criticism. Of course, it can be said that this is how all good teaching is accomplished. I agree, but I also have to recognize that specialization has now reached such a point that many graduates, even good ones, seem to be ignorant outside their own subject; alternatively, they are without deep knowledge of any subject Organizationally, I believe that every faculty should provide not only teachers of subjects, but supervisors. Supervisors should preferably cover more than one subject; ideally, they should be able to range over the whole course, so that a student could retain the same supervisor throughout his stay in the institution.

This would mean that in each faculty managing system there would appear a control and service function called 'supervision'; it would consist of supervisors, each of whom would be responsible for what might be called the intellectual training of a group of students.

The intakes into the supervising system are the same as those of an institution whose primary task is instruction – the untaught and the untrained. But the criteria for the judgement of performance differ. The questions asked as a result of the conversion activities would be: 'How well does he think?' rather than 'How much does he know?' and 'What is his capacity for learning?' rather than 'What has he learned?'

GROWTH AND MATURATION

The difficulties caused by the explosion of knowledge, and the consequent rapid increase in specialization and fragmentation, go, I believe, much deeper. Any university has the task of producing the next generation of the leaders of its society. I use 'leader' in its widest sense. To me, a scholar discovering new knowledge, or new meaning in what is already known, is taking a leadership role, as is the builder of an industrial empire, the creator of a new industry, a politician introducing new policies, or an officer serving in the armed forces. With the rapid expansion of higher education it is unlikely that future leaders will not have passed through its institutions. Whatever else they do, universities educate the intellectual elite of their societies. Provided they do not regress into ivory towers, isolated from their environment – and it is remarkable how long a university can survive by doing so – they can hardly help but have a profound effect on future leaders. The important question is: What kinds of leader will the society of the future require? And, perhaps more painfully: Have the present leaders the skill and the knowledge to design educational processes that will produce the new kinds of leader required? Are students to be encouraged to model themselves on their present leaders, or are they to be given opportunities to grow and to mature, to decide for themselves what beliefs they will hold, what traditions they will respect and what they will discard? Are they to model themselves on those who have failed to solve the world's problems, or are they to be encouraged to become new leaders who will be innovative, creative, and producers of change?

If, at one extreme, society wants conservative traditionalists, then educational institutions should discourage change and innovation, and encourage conformity and passivity. The congruent culture is repressive, regimented, and dictatorial. If society wants creative innovators, then educational institutions must encourage experiment and change, and discourage conformity and passivity – in themselves as institutions as much as, if not more than, elsewhere. The congruent culture is permissive, flexible, and democratic. But, and it is an important 'but', a culture that is wholly permissive, wholly flexible, and so democratic that nothing can be done without the consent of the majority, is one that inevitably degenerates into promiscuity, flabbiness, and futility. There are plenty of models for turning out the leaders and followers of a regimented society; and many of today's universities provide models of what happens when permissiveness becomes promiscuity, flexibility becomes flabbiness, and democracy degenerates into futility. I shall concern myself with a model for an institution that offers opportunities for maturation and growth within boundaries that protect the students while they experiment with their opportunities; an institution in which young men and women can learn not only to make their own decisions (for that is what the leaders have to do) but also to accept the consequences of those decisions.

By growth and maturation I mean the process of acquiring some capacity to distinguish between fantasy and reality, some basis upon which to decide what experience and knowledge to accept and what to discard, what beliefs and attitudes to incorporate into, and what to reject from, the values that underlie behaviour. The problem for any institution is how to secure the commitment of its members to its goals and objectives – so that all its members, at whatever level, can feel free to express their views without prejudice to their careers, and yet they will remain committed should some decision go against them.

The intakes into the system are the inexperienced and immature; the conversion processes are the opportunities for them to mature, to experiment, to rehearse; the outputs are those who have taken advantage of their opportunities, and those who have not. Growth and maturation cannot be 'taught'. Members of the faculty may provide models of mature behaviour; they may guide and advise; they may, or should, be able to set limits to experiment and protect their students from unwarranted interference from other authorities; but they cannot teach maturation in any conventional sense. The epitome of failure is when the faculty has to call in external authority, for example, the police, to maintain or to attempt to re-establish its own authority.

The essential task system is again, as for teaching and supervision, a member of the faculty and the students for whose growth and maturation he is primarily responsible. For convenience, and to remain within academic nomenclature, I refer to the role of the staff member in this system as 'tutor'. In the sense in which I use the title, the tutor is a member of the academic faculty who may, or may not (preferably not), also teach or supervise in the academic discipline that his students (those to whom he is tutor) are following.

It goes without saying that a tutor must be primarily interested in his students as growing and developing human beings. This is not to say that he will not be concerned with their intellectual and academic achievements, since such achievements are part of their growing process, and are more than likely to affect their future lives. But his task is rather to help them to decide for themselves what courses to take, and how much effort and attention to give to courses in relation to other available activities. A tutor's job is to advise and counsel, rather than to order. At the same time, the tutor should have the authority, on the one hand, to place limits on student behaviour, and, on the other, to protect students from other kinds of authority, both academic and external, that he deems unsuitable. Furthermore, he should not hesitate to exercise his authority. The tutor, in effect, gives his students opportunities to experiment in a transitional situation – between that of teenagers under the control of parents and that of independent adults responsible to themselves. To do this, he needs to provide a model of adult behaviour that can cope not only with problems of education but also with problems of authority and responsibility in a rapidly changing environment.

In a residential university, the tutor can be most effective in what might be termed the 'living', as distinct from the 'working', process – teaching and supervision. In a non-residential university his influence is inevitably likely to be less, but I believe that such a role and task system are still essential.

To the model organization of *Figure 13* should therefore be added a further operating system (or systems) headed by tutors. This is shown in *Figure 14*. (Supervisory functions are also shown.) Organizationally, the management of the tutorial system can be carried out by a senior tutor or by the tutors as a group. To me, the important point is that this is a separate yet interdependent part of the educational institution. Since tutors, as tutors, are primarily interested in their students as human beings, the model of adult behaviour they set, and the system to which they belong, should be consistent with the culture of the environment in which the students will have to live.

In other words, tutors should always have other working roles (which could even be extra-mural). At all costs, tutoring should avoid becoming still another specialization. If specialized counselling is required to deal with breakdowns, this is the task of specialists in a different service, for example, the student health service. It is not the task of the tutor in the educational system. The tutoring techniques used – group or individual meetings, or any other methods – will be determined by the skill and experience of the tutors, and, of course, by their students. And the number of students to a tutor will

FIGURE 14 *Model organization for a simplified educational institution*

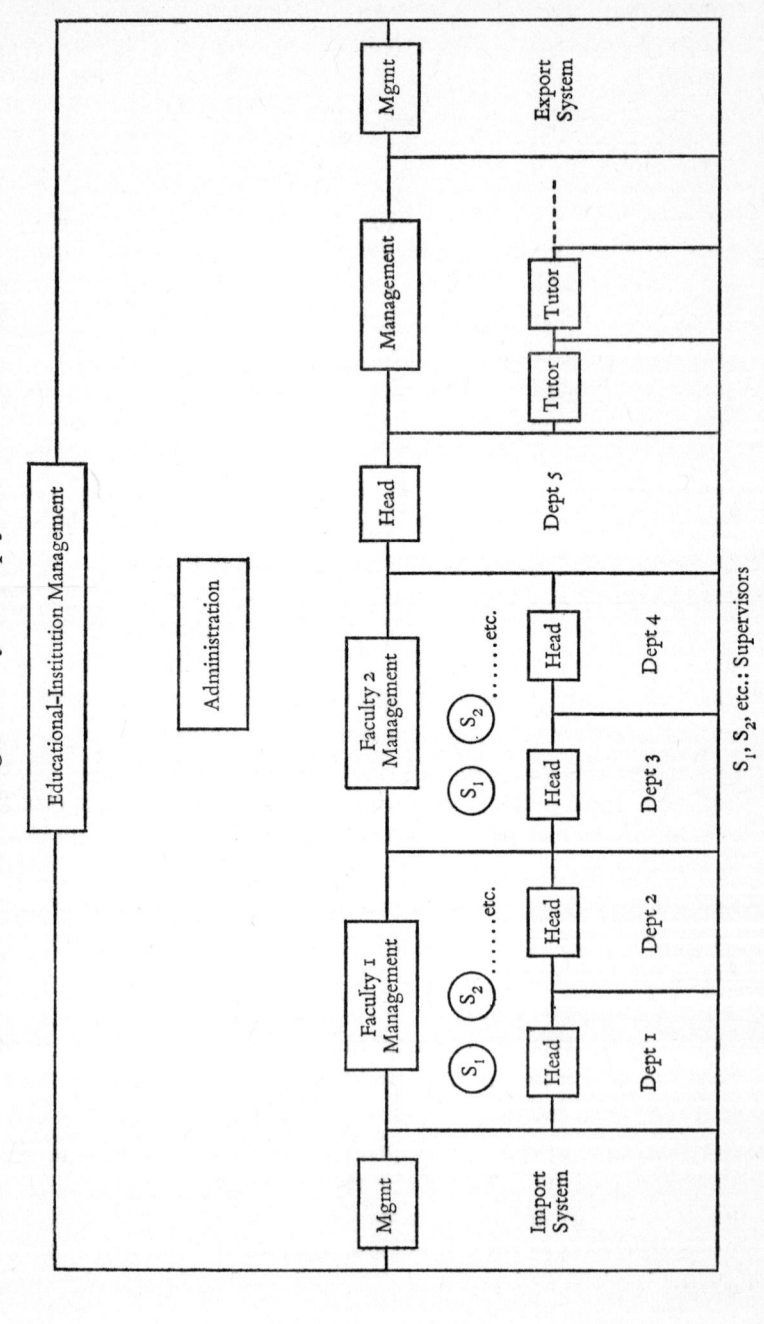

S_1, S_2, etc.: Supervisors

MODEL FOR TASK PERFORMANCE: EDUCATION

depend on how many each tutor feels able to cope with. I suggest, however, that two points deserve consideration:

(a) while it is obvious that the group should not be so large that the tutor cannot know his students intimately, it should not be so small that it is too closely identified with a family group;

(b) group and individual meetings should not be held so frequently that they become just another chore for both tutor and students.

Both points are designed to guard against a tendency to encourage over-determined dependency in the students, and perhaps against a willingness, on the part of the faculty, to go into collusion with the over-determination.

CHAPTER 6

A Model Organization for Undergraduate Education

The process of education in all universities provides a major discontinuity at graduation. All of them differentiate undergraduates and graduates. In addition, many universities today take instruction to be the primary task of undergraduate education; and research or professional training to be the tasks of postgraduate education. The implied assumption is that graduation marks, not only a definite academic boundary, but also a boundary in the student's maturation. As he crosses this boundary the student moves from being a young person to being an adult. Unfortunately, the increasing number of students demanding, and being offered, opportunities for higher education has so stretched most universities' resources that many undergraduate teaching institutions have become more akin to factories than to educational institutions. Their raw materials are matriculates, their outputs graduates and dropouts. In this factory process, the discovery of knowledge, intellectual training, and the provision of opportunities for growth and maturation have been relegated to such minor tasks that in some universities they have almost disappeared.

The same process has devalued the first degrees awarded at graduation. They are rapidly becoming worthless as academic qualifications. Only the acquisition of a second and higher degree confers academic respectability. (And it can be suggested that if second degrees continue to be awarded at the current rate, a third degree will soon be required.) But this devaluation of the first degree and the consequent necessity for a second also blur the distinction between undergraduate and postgraduate education. Indeed, in some universities students are continuing to be referred to as undergraduates until they have obtained their PH.D or equivalent professional qualification. There is, for example, a growing tendency, particularly in the United

States, to prescribe detailed courses as requirements for a PH.D degree. A corollary is that both faculty (and society) tend to treat postgraduate students as immature, even though biologically and chronologically they are adult.

If the tasks of intellectual training and of providing opportunities for growth and maturation are not undertaken by the university, either the tasks are left undone or other agencies and institutions have to perform them. Families, student unions and clubs, and other social and political activities all have their natural part to play, but I postulate that if the university, as the primary institution in an undergraduate's life, does not play its part, then task performance must remain incomplete. If the university does not provide intellectual training and adequate opportunities for growth and maturation, it is offering a model of an institution whose leaders fail to assume some of their major responsibilities and fail to exercise important aspects of their authority. Moreover, the same university leadership frequently offers a model of adult authority that responds only punitively when the students, perhaps not unnaturally, protest.

I could go further and suggest that many of the disciplinary measures introduced into courses – compulsory attendance at classes, excessive testing and grading – about which students so frequently protest, are attempts to reinforce an authority lost because of its failure to accept responsibility either for intellectual training or for the provision of opportunities for growth and maturation. The conclusion can only be that any model organization for undergraduate education should provide for the performance of at least three tasks: instruction, intellectual training, and the provision of opportunities for growth and maturation. If all three are not included at undergraduate level, then steps should be taken to make up the deficiencies at postgraduate level. In a very general sense, universities can be said to be concerned with the discovery of knowledge: what the undergraduate 'discovers' is usually already known; what the postgraduate 'discovers' is less often so. But both undergraduates and postgraduates have to discover for themselves to what use they can put the knowledge they gain, and they have to accept responsibility for such use. This, after all, is what growth and maturation are about.

THE ACTIVITIES OF UNDERGRADUATE EDUCATION

In Chapter 5 I suggested that, while intellectual training was part of good teaching, it could be regarded organizationally as a separate task that required special supervisory functions in the managing system. In discussing a model for undergraduate education, therefore, I refer to three parallel processes, of which two, instruction and supervision, are included in the teaching system and the third, the provision of opportunities for growth and maturation, is in the tutorial system. A simplified representation of the import-conversion-export systems for a standard three-year course is shown in *Figure 15*. The intakes and outputs of all three processes are the same: matriculates who become graduates (or dropouts and failures); the untrained who are trained; the immature who mature.

FIGURE 15 *The import-conversion-export processes of undergraduate education*

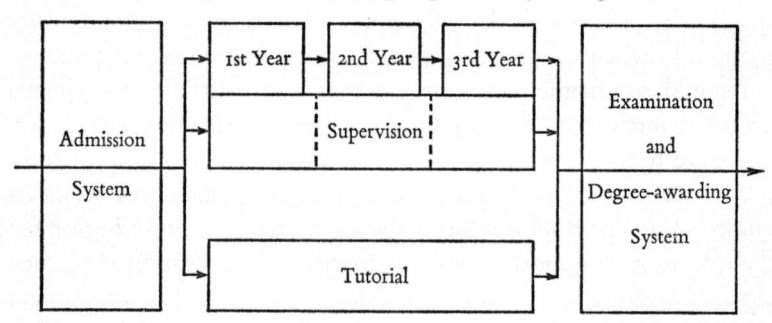

In the instruction system four discontinuities are shown: at entry, between the first and second years, between the second and third years, and at graduation. Not all these discontinuities are necessary, but at undergraduate level some intervening discontinuity between matriculation and graduation is probably desirable, if only to let the undergraduate know how he is getting on.

In the supervision system possible discontinuities are shown. They may or may not coincide in time with those of the instruction system, and the student may or may not require as many supervisors as he has subjects. Preferably, he should keep the same supervisors throughout his undergraduate career and one supervisor should be able to deal with more than one subject in order to avoid, as far as is

MODEL ORGANIZATION FOR UNDERGRADUATE EDUCATION

possible, the fragmentation of instruction due to over-specialization. The primary task of the system is to help the student to think for himself. He should he encouraged to criticize the instruction he is getting, to question the texts he is expected to read, and to prepare work for criticism by his supervisor. With his supervisor he should be able to discuss which classes he should attend and which he might profitably skip.

In the tutorial system no discontinuities are shown. Except when the relationship between a particular tutor and a particular student becomes intolerable, the student should keep the same tutor throughout. The primary task of this system is to offer opportunities for growth and maturation. It is with his tutor that the student can discuss any difficulties he may have with his teachers and supervisors, and his attitudes towards his course, the university, and authority in general. The tutor is concerned with the student's total behaviour rather than with his academic performance. It is therefore irrelevant whether the tutor shares the student's discipline or not. But I have suggested that preferably he should not. This will avoid the tutorial system taking on, or supplementing, the task of the supervisory system; and, more importantly, the tutor can provide still another model of an adult role.

The appropriate organizational model for all these processes has been shown in simplified form in *Figure 14* of Chapter 5. Before this model is elaborated, two further points need consideration: the effects of university expansion, and the case for research work in the undergraduate system.

UNIVERSITY EXPANSION

In most residential universities in which the tutorial system exists, it is linked to colleges, dormitories, or halls of residence. Even where there is no tutorial system as elaborate as that I have described, a warden or some similar official is expected to take a kind of tutorial role. I suggest that in the majority of residential universities and in almost all non-residential universities the role has not been accorded the importance it warrants.

In those residential universities in which the tutorial system has been attached to the colleges in which undergraduates live, irrespective of the courses they are studying, the difficulty has been the relative power of colleges, faculties, departments, and overall university management. Many believe that in the older universities of the United Kingdom the colleges have too much power, and university management and faculties have too little. Where colleges have been reduced to halls of residence (whatever name they have gone by, and even with a tutorial system), the power and status of the halls, and of their wardens and tutors, have been too little to counterbalance the power of faculties and departments. In these circumstances the provision of opportunities for growth and maturation has usually degenerated into a narrow function of maintaining discipline. Students at many such universities have, not unnaturally, responded unfavourably to a process that has seemed to them to be negatively restrictive rather than positively educational. In some newer universities, mixed housing for faculty and students has been provided. But this solution has succeeded only in separating the faculty into generations: the unmarried and the newly married faculty may live in such quarters; those who have families tend to move away. In such universities the tendency has been for junior faculty to identify with students in opposition to their senior colleagues.

The general point I wish to make is about the change that has occurred mainly as a result of the expansion of facilities for higher education. When universities were, in reality, comparatively small communities of scholars, all three tasks – instruction, intellectual training, and the provision of opportunities for growth and maturation – were performed by the same system. Task and hence role differentiation were unimportant and unnecessary. As universities became larger, the undergraduates, on whose throughput an undergraduate educational system depends, found it more and more difficult to identify with the whole community, and some more easily identifiable groupings became necessary. The denigration of the 'living' system, represented by tutorials, as against the 'working' system, represented by instruction, left only one institutional choice: identification with faculty or department. But the working system was not designed primarily to provide opportunities for growth and maturation, and so this essential task has not been performed, even by universities that have resisted letting classes grow to the point of gross impersonalization.

MODEL ORGANIZATION FOR UNDERGRADUATE EDUCATION

Since the universities have failed to make adequate provision for the process of growth and maturation, it is perhaps hardly surprising that the students have made their own. And, in the uncertain conditions of the modern world, it is not surprising that the groupings provided by the students should have furnished a fertile ground for political and social protest, often accompanied by the violence and destructiveness that are characteristic of immaturity. But do not let me suggest that this is all it is. In a later chapter I shall discuss some of the problems and myths connected with 'participation in decision-making'. At this point I would note only that it is my belief that the comparatively small groups of student activists are acting not only on behalf of the vast majority of students, but on behalf of many faculty members as well, even those who in their official capacities deny any such identification. By projecting their protest and potential destructiveness into minorities, they can deny their own ambivalence, or, at worst, their collusion.

THE CASE FOR RESEARCH AT UNDERGRADUATE LEVEL

By its very nature, education is a change process: it changes, or is supposed to change, its throughput, the students. The environment in which most education takes place is also changing, and at an ever-increasing rate. It is unlikely, therefore, that members of the faculty, or students for that matter, can ignore, without serious distortion of the educational process, innovation and change either in the definition of their tasks or in the methods of their performance. But if innovation and change are to be controlled and directed, rather than random and chaotic, then research (with research management) is required – at least into ways of improving the educational process.

I have tried, for example, to make a strong case for what I have called the tutorial system as an essential part of the educational process. I do not pretend, however, that the setting up of tutors who see their students occasionally, or even frequently, will of itself establish an adequate system for the provision of opportunities for growth and maturation. If tutors can be found who, while taking a genuine interest in their students as developing human beings, do not avoid problems of the exercise of authority, they can provide adult models with whom the students can identify. But without more understanding of the problems of growth and maturation in contemporary society, the provision of adult models whose behaviour is based on established tradition is unlikely to be enough. 'Group dynamics', whatever form it takes, and I do not wish to argue here for any particular form, has at least demonstrated that there are methods whereby people can be given opportunities to 'rehearse' the many different ways in which leadership roles can be taken, and to learn something of the way in which their own behaviour affects others, and others' behaviour affects their own. Scientifically and academically speaking, group dynamics, or any other name given to its many different forms, is still very new and unproven. Student counselling is not universally practised, and, where it is, it is not much more than an attempt to serve those who have broken down so badly as to require specialized psychiatric help. Even psychiatry itself is not yet considered by some universities to be academically respectable.

Research into educational processes seems, therefore, essential. But I would go further and suggest that action research into the place of the university in contemporary society is also essential. Action research into student disorders, for instance, would perhaps help students to choose their targets with more discrimination, and to protest more effectively. At the very least, if the activities of faculty and students are to be subject to research, then they are likely to respond with more understanding and insight if they too can take part in research activities.

A MODEL ORGANIZATION FOR AN UNDERGRADUATE EDUCATIONAL INSTITUTION

The Operating Systems

If I now put together the model organizations I have developed for research (*Figure 7*) and teaching (*Figure 14*), the first- and second-order operating systems appear as in *Figure 16*. For simplicity, I have omitted independent departments that provide courses in more than one faculty, on the assumptions, first, that with a large number of faculties there are likely to be few such departments, and, second, that students who require subjects belonging to other faculties will be accommodated in them. I realize also that as soon as I introduce the whole range of research activities I am begging the question of post-

FIGURE 16 *First- and second-order operating systems of an institution for undergraduate education*

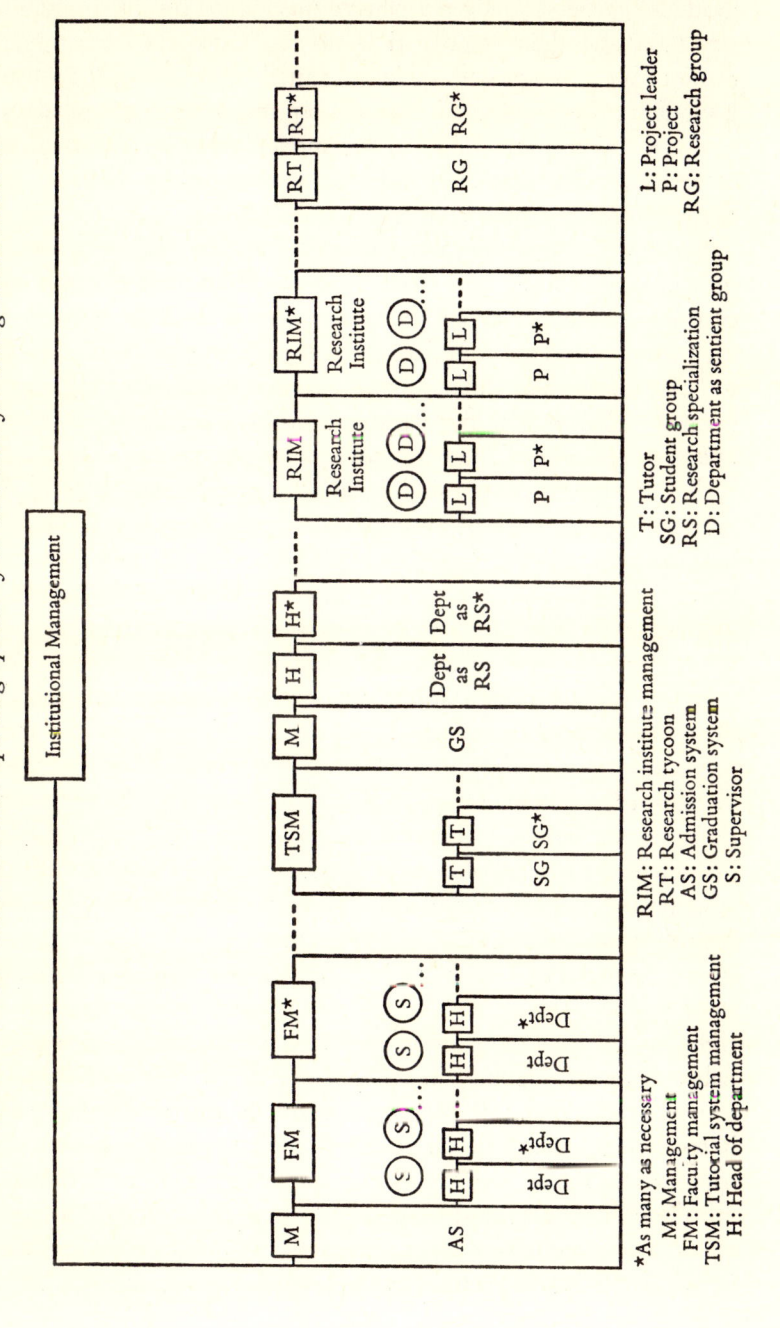

graduate participation, but I believe that the complexity of university tasks and their organization will be more comprehensible if some of the consequences of the potential confusion of task-system boundaries are considered before postgraduate research and professional training are added to the model. After all, there are still some universities that cater only for undergraduate education, and many in which professional training does not exist in any form.

Even with these simplifications the model demonstrates the difficulties that could arise from the opportunities for multiple role-carrying by the faculty, on the one hand, and from the corresponding opportunities for boundary confusion, on the other. It is a cliché to point to the many different roles that every individual takes in his normal daily life. It is so usual that most people are not consciously aware of changes of role. But roles belong to task systems and, as such, carry specific responsibilities and require the exercise of appropriate authority. Lack of awareness of change of role can therefore lead to confusion of responsibility and authority. To put this another way: if an individual is not aware when he crosses a boundary from one task system to another, he may be unaware of the changes in structure and culture to which he must adjust.

In the model organization, for example, it can be seen that discipline-based departments appear as parts of faculties in the teaching system, that is, they are second-order systems. They also appear as first-order systems in research; and as control and service functions in the second-order managing system required by research institutes. A member of a department could have roles in all three systems. He could teach undergraduates, conduct research in his own speciality, and be a member of a project team (and hence of a sentient group) in a research institute. He could also act as a faculty supervisor and as a tutor, and be either a research tycoon in his own right or a member of a tycoon's research group. And he would probably have no difficulty in recognizing the change in task, as he moved from role to role. When it is a senior member of a faculty who is concerned, however, he is called upon to display considerable sophistication if he is to recognize, and accept, that his authority is not the same in all roles; he is only too apt to use the authority he enjoys in the highest-order system to distort and disrupt the systems in which he has less authority. It is often equally difficult for his juniors in one system to oppose him in others in which his authority is structurally the same as or less than theirs; they may be too dependent on him for their future careers.

There is no purely organizational solution to such problems. Attempts to delineate responsibilities by laying down, for example, how many hours per week each faculty member must teach, or how many papers he must publish each year, seldom provide anything but irritation for the competent and alibis for the incompetent. Equally, a plethora of committees set up to coordinate tasks and roles at every level only too frequently wastes the time of those who have real work to do and provides apparent occupation for those who have not. Solutions have to be behavioural as well as organizational. This means that institutional management must exercise authority to reinforce appropriate behaviour, and to take remedial action whenever faculty behaviour does not match role and task. If an important task of a university is to provide models of mature adult behaviour, then members of the faculty should demonstrate that it is possible to take different roles, accepting the responsibilities and exercising the authority appropriate to each one. And they should have the opportunity to do this with dignity and integrity. And this in turn means that the institution itself should provide a model of a sophisticated and integrated multiple-task institution, in which the claims of different tasks are adequately balanced. This is not to say that there should not be conflicts between the leaders of different tasks, or alternative leaders of the same task, but that the conflicts should be between the right roles and about the right things.

So far, I have been considering the operating systems that, from the theoretical point of view, would be required to perform the teaching and research tasks of an institution for undergraduate education. I have previously argued, however, that in a university of any size it is difficult for the student to identify continuously with the whole, and that even with a tutorial system some intermediate grouping between the large whole and the small tutorial group is required. I have also argued the interdependence of teaching and research in a dynamic institution.

The theoretical model of *Figure 16* does not provide the intermediate groups with which students can identify. I suggest, therefore, that whether a university is residential or not, some form of 'collegiate' differentiation is essential, and that the 'colleges' must not only be related to the 'living' process as distinct from the 'working' process, and hence incorporate the tutorial system, but also have sufficient status in the institution to balance the power of the research 'working' system represented by faculties and departments. Obviously it is easier to achieve this in a residential than in a non-residential setting, but failure to provide an adequate 'living' system means that the university is abdicating responsibility for one of its important tasks.

In spite of what I have written about the need for sophisticated behaviour in recognizing different roles taken in different task systems, I doubt whether, in practice, it is possible for the members of a discipline-based department to separate their functions of teaching and research to the extent that they recognize a different organization and administrative procedure and different institutionalized leadership in the two systems. I suggest, therefore, that in practice discipline-based departments in faculties for the tasks of teaching and research should be amalgamated in the teaching system.

The Managing System

Before putting these two modifications into the model – colleges in the 'living' system and the amalgamation of teaching and discipline-based research in discipline-based departments – I have to turn attention to the differentiated functions of the managing system.

The managing system of institutional management has to provide both appropriate control and service functions to manage the university and appropriate sentient groups for faculty and students where these do not exist. If 'colleges' exist, or can be set up, and not only undergraduates and their tutors, but postgraduate students and other faculty, are attached to them, they can provide powerful sentient groups – too powerful, many believe, in the universities of Oxford and Cambridge. The question then arises whether colleges, faculties, and research institutes provide adequate participation (and hence sentience) for both faculty and students (the original community of scholars) in the formulation and implementation of university policy, as distinct from college, faculty, or institute policy. Contemporary events suggest that they do not, even at those universities where the college system is highly developed. It should nevertheless be noted that large universities that have no collegiate system appear to have suffered far more disorder than those that have such a system. I therefore suggest that the managing system should also contain task-oriented sentient groups for both faculty and students. Their function would be to provide faculty and students with opportunities to discuss, and to contribute to, university policy. The actual form of these sentient groups should be left to faculty and students. An obvious differentiation is by grades for faculty and by years for students, but there are many other possible groupings. Though I suggest that appropriate sentient groups should be 'institutionalized', that is, should be recognized as official contributors to university policy-making, I would deplore the common habit of rushing to rigid constitution-building: deciding how many representatives of what grade or year should sit on a common council; wrangling about voting rights and voting procedures; and all the other tangles that such deliberations can only too readily produce. To me the important point is that the system should permit all voices to be heard, and not only those representing majority votes. Innovation, creativity, and education for that matter, are seldom the result of political democratic processes. In a teaching and research culture, the minority 'voice', even the lone 'voice', may contain the greater truth, and there should be mechanisms to ensure that it is heard.

In addition to the sentient groups, the first-order managing system will have to include as many differentiated control and service functions as are necessary for the running of the institution. For the purposes of the model, I include a library, financial control, administration, a personnel function, and, for want of a better term, two general service functions. I am thinking here of such things as data-processing, building and plant maintenance, and the like. The modified model is shown in *Figure 17*.

I suppose the first thing I should emphasize is that *Figure 17* does not define status (nor do any other of the diagrams, for that matter). I do not think that all operating systems need to be of equal importance, or that all of their managements need to have equal rank. But this does not mean that they should not be first-order systems. So far as they are engaged in different tasks, use different resources, and have different throughputs, they have to be organizationally differentiated. But that one may be large and another small does not mean that the latter should be subordinate to the former. The same is true of the control and service functions and of the sentient groups. The inclusion of all categories of faculty and students in the first-order managing system, for instance, does not imply that they all have the same status or the same rights to determine policy. Clearly they have not; but it does imply that that is the level at which their sentience has to be taken into account. More importantly, perhaps, it places an obligation on management to make explicit just how much notice it takes of the views of the various groups, and just how much time it is prepared to spend in 'participation'. It should also be noted that the inclusion of all these categories in the first-order system allows institutional management to spend as much time as is necessary with whichever group, at any specific time, happens to be the most troublesome, or the most powerful, without transgressing its own organizational boundaries.

In the first-order managing system in *Figure 17* I have also shown the possibility of the formation of a council or councils composed of representatives of, or of all members of, sentient groups and of institutional management. I have shown it in this way to emphasize two points: first, that its formation (or not) is something for the sentient groups to decide; and, second, that, even if it is formed, it cannot, without the agreement of all the sentient groups, abrogate their right of direct access to institutional management. The key point is that each member of the faculty and each student should have more than one role, and more than one route, through which he can make his voice heard. Only with multiple roles and multiple routes available are different shades of opinion and different views about different parts of the institutional complex likely to be heard.

With all that said, however, I have to admit that the first-order managing system contains such a large number that it could well result in a Babel of 'voices'. In practice, mechanisms may have to be designed to simplify procedures for making views known. To some extent the success of such procedures depends on the nature of, and the leadership given by, institutional management, and on the nature of, and the leadership given by, the management of the many different operating systems. I propose to discuss these problems

FIGURE 17 *Modified organizational model for the first-order systems of an institution for undergraduate education*

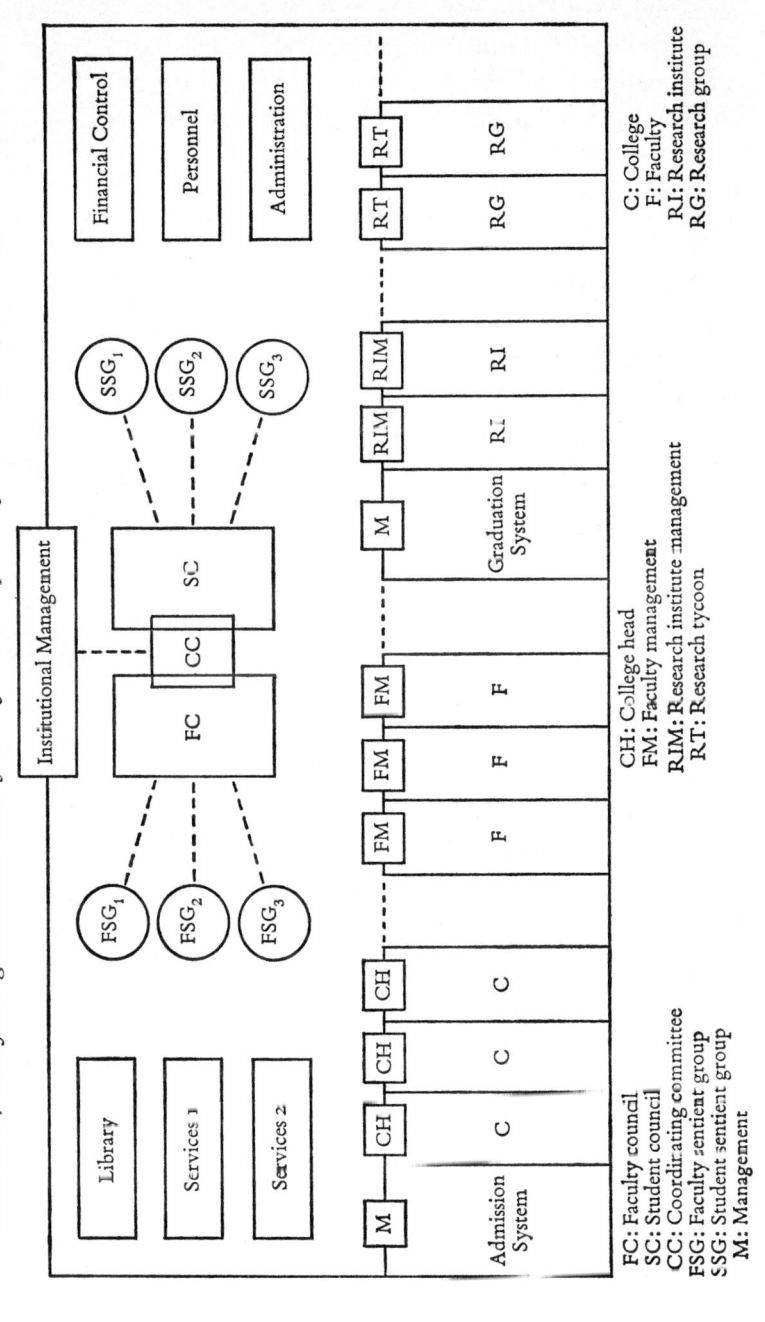

FC: Faculty council
SC: Student council
CC: Coordinating committee
FSG: Faculty sentient group
SSG: Student sentient group
M: Management

CH: College head
FM: Faculty management
RIM: Research institute management
RT: Research tycoon

C: College
F: Faculty
RI: Research institute
RG: Research group

more fully in Chapter 10 when I come to university governance. Here I should like to stress two points that I have already made in other contexts: first, that a box representing 'management' need not be filled by only one person; and, second, that though members of the faculty inevitably provide models of individual adult behaviour, the institution itself should also provide a model of sophisticated organizational behaviour. A managing system comprising a large number of members should not be avoided as an organizational *principle*. The members' inability to think in a large meeting, containing overlapping and interdependent interests, may inhibit debate, but the inhibition is a constraint, and the constraint may require compromise, or the creation of devices to enable real debate to take place. A sophisticated organization is inventive of such devices and is prepared to experiment with them; furthermore, it is sufficiently flexible to make changes when experiment shows that its procedures are not achieving its objectives.

CHAPTER 7

Postgraduate Education

RESEARCH

In postgraduate education I include education for research work in all fields of knowledge, and professional training of all kinds. In Chapter 4 I discussed some of the organizational problems of university research, pointing particularly to the distinction between traditional research work, either tycoon- or discipline-based, and problem-centred multidisciplinary research. I suggested that in modern conditions more room had to be found for problem-centred multidisciplinary research, offering more practical payoffs for its sponsors, and that this implied a diminution in the power of the traditional discipline-based departments. I also drew attention to the confusion that would ensue for both faculty and students with regard to the teaching of research methodology and the finding of research problems suitable for young, untried postgraduates.

I concluded that those postgraduate students whose primary objective was a doctorate would fare better in discipline-based departments whose primary task was teaching. I also concluded that university research would be more effective if it were organized in differentiated systems with different primary tasks: support for genuinely creative workers, research institutes for problem-centred research, discipline-based departments for narrowly based specialization, and teaching departments to provide opportunities for postgraduate students to learn research methodology and to acquire higher degrees. Then, in Chapter 6, when discussing the place of research in an institution for undergraduate education, I amalgamated the third and fourth systems into one research and teaching category as a practical compromise. I mentioned some of the difficulties consequent upon the explosion of knowledge and the increased demand for higher education, including those that are likely to arise (and indeed have arisen) when second degrees are no longer considered to confer special academic merit, and still higher qualifications have to be acquired. This question I propose to take up again in the next two chapters. In this chapter I wish to build the organizational model for postgraduate education and also to draw attention to the increasing confusion between research work and professional training.

Up to the second world war, research workers in the natural sciences at least could claim that they were discovering new knowledge and that no 'professional' element was required in their training. With the development of nuclear physics, and the resulting atomic and hydrogen weapons, many of them have been forced on to the defensive about their work, and have disclaimed responsibility for the use that is made of their discoveries. More recently, particularly in America, students (and some faculty) have gone much further and have declared that it is immoral for universities to accept research contracts from government departments concerned with the armed forces. Such people sometimes appear to behave as though they believed that just changing the source of the contract would somehow ensure that discoveries would be used only for peaceful purposes: for the benefit, rather than the destruction, of mankind. I have already indicated that I believe this to be a forlorn hope, and that apparently the most beneficial of inventions can lead to man's destruction if man does not learn to control their application. And this means that man has to learn to control himself.

In the biological and social sciences, and in the humanities, the relationship of research work to contemporary human problems is much clearer; but so, by the same token, is there greater confusion between what is research work and what professional training. This has led to two major consequences:

(a) the closer the research work has been related to a contemporary problem of the individual, the group, or the community, the more it has had to be broken down into 'harmless' elements so that junior research workers could work on them without risk to themselves or to the source of their data;

(b) for their own protection, those scientists who could assert that their work had only indirect and distant relationships with a contemporary problem have claimed, like the natural scientist, to be in 'basic' research, and to be 'purer' than their 'applied' or 'clinical' colleagues.

I believe that these consequences largely explain the existing conflict between the 'pure' and 'applied' sciences, and much of what I have somewhat rudely called 'the premature measurement of the irrelevant' that goes on in the social sciences. I also believe that they account for much of the student dissatisfaction with the role that universities are playing in the modern world.

The organization for teaching postgraduate students to carry out research has already been given in Chapter 4. May I repeat that, so far as is possible, research students wanting to learn research methodology and to acquire a higher degree are best located in discipline-based departments. Those who obtain posts in problem-centred research institutes or become members of a tycoon's research group are there to contribute to the work of the respective institute or group; any thesis they may write, or any degree they may acquire, is a by-product – the result of the performance of a secondary, not a primary, task of the institute or group.

PROFESSIONAL TRAINING

The essential characteristics of a profession are that its practice is required by its society; and that society has delegated to the members of the profession the responsibility and authority to determine both the minimum qualifications of its practitioners and the standards of behaviour to which they will adhere. Strictly speaking, therefore, professional education involves not only extended instruction beyond graduation, but practice under supervision as well. The intakes into the system are graduates (or those with equivalent qualifications); the conversion processes are the teaching of theory and practice; and the outputs are qualified practitioners. I recognize that I am ignoring what could be called professional training at the undergraduate level or its equivalent, for example in engineering or architecture. I do so, not because I believe it to be unimportant, but because I believe that what I have argued earlier about undergraduate education applies with equal force to any education at that level, including vocational education in university, technical college, or polytechnic.

Not all professional education is carried out in universities. Much, if not most of it, is conducted by the professional bodies to which society has delegated its authority; and the professional bodies govern to some extent both curricula for instruction and examinations that confer qualification. Those responsible for professional education in universities always therefore have ties with, and usually loyalties to, other institutions than the university or school in which they teach. A university may distrust such divided loyalty, and it would be surprising if those members of the academic faculty whose whole career is dependent on 'academic' qualifications were not sometimes envious of the additional degree of freedom enjoyed by their professional colleagues.

Moreover, teachers of professions, according to my definition, have to teach practice as well as theory. Until new teaching techniques are developed, much of the learning has to be by apprenticeship, and, if the teachers are to retain the respect of their students, this means that they have to practise themselves. The relationship between teacher and taught is powerfully reinforced by the harsh test that such practice provides. Those who survive this test are often regarded with considerable jealousy, however unconscious, by those whose discipline does not give them the opportunity to undergo it – particularly if they fear that they would not survive it if it did.

At the same time, survival of the harsh test of practice can so reinforce the relationship between teacher and student that the student is tempted into over-identification with his teacher, a process that is still more reinforced if what I have called the task of providing opportunities for growth and maturation is not adequately performed at the undergraduate level. This problem is particularly acute in what are now called the 'helping' professions. Owing to the nature of the tasks undertaken, the culture within these professions, and between their practitioners and those to whom they offer help, is dependent. In the medical profession, perhaps the most extreme example, patients have to depend on doctors for treatment; they literally put their lives in doctors' hands. They depend on the doctor's devotion to his professional code of conduct to ensure that his power will not be abused. Both the dependent culture and the practice encourage identification and imitation; but it has to be recognized that identification and imitation can inhibit innovation in a rapidly changing field.

The same problem, but in a different form, confronts those postgraduate educational institutions – whether they are attached to universities or are independent – that are teaching what has not yet attained the status of a true profession. Business schools and institutes of management are perhaps the best examples. There are no generally recognized external bodies to give sanction to their courses or their examinations; and there are few established relationships with external institutions to facilitate practice under supervision (as medical schools have hospitals). Except in the school or institute itself, there is nowhere for the students to watch their teachers in action as practising managers. Members of the faculty can maintain some of their own skills by practising consultancy, either individually or collectively, and such practice can enrich their teaching and their research. But it is rare for them to be able to introduce their students into their practices. And consultancy is not what they are employed to teach.

Finally, there are the professions, such as law, architecture, divinity, or the arts, in which the teaching of practice, as well as of theory, can be conducted in private. In other words, apprenticeship can be postponed until the students leave the university. Members of the faculties of these professions do not have to practise in the public arena, and thus expose themselves to public scrutiny (as, for example, the clinical members of a medical school faculty have to do). As against this, however, those who spend all their time in teaching and research are not infrequently felt by their students, as well as by their practising colleagues, to have avoided many of the harsh tests that professional practice involves.

I can only conclude, then, that if universities are to take seriously the task of professional training, a subject to which I shall return in the next chapter, it is very desirable that opportunities for practice under supervision should be provided. Without opportunities for practice, the essentially 'professional' part of the training is not carried out, and the university is concerned only with pre-professional education. But if practice in some form is to be included in the training, then an additional interdependent task is added to the tasks of teaching and research, which I have argued are the essential interdependent tasks of university institutions. The addition of the third task – practice – makes it unlikely that the kind of organization, and the status and value systems, that are appropriate to undergraduate and postgraduate research education will still be appropriate for professional training. To take a simple example: whereas it may be possible, in a normal university faculty appointment, to suggest that a candidate should show excellence in research and outstanding competence in teaching, or vice versa (although, to judge by many reports, teaching ability does not appear to have had a very high priority in many university appointments), it is surely asking too much to insist on excellence or even outstanding competence in the performance of three tasks. What so frequently happens is that the need for competence in all three tasks is acknowledged, but performance in one of them is valued more highly than performance in the others. The consequences are imbalance in the system and, in present-day conditions, protest from those who suffer as a result of the lesser competence: the students being taught, the community being practised upon, or the sponsors of the research.

A different task, and a different kind of organization, require a different kind of institution. For convenience, I propose to call this a 'School' – a term common in many universities. Schools require three major types of operating system: for teaching, for research, and for practice. A school management will need to control three major kinds of boundary transaction: with the community within which the school practises; with the university of which it is a part and through which it gets support, and which will set standards of teaching and research; and, internally, between the different kinds of operating system, each with its own (different) criteria for the judgement of performance. An outline organization of the operating systems is shown in *Figure 18*. Comparison of *Figure 18* with *Figure 16* demonstrates how easily confusion can arise between the two organizations. A school is likely to require discipline-based departments to teach the sciences appropriate to its profession. Such departments are likely to have the same name and to employ the same skills as are found in similar departments in other parts of the university; but teaching theory to a student who is going to practise is not necessarily the same task as teaching it to one who is not. For the same reason, research work in a practising school is, or should be, slanted towards application rather than towards the discovery of knowledge for its own sake. I am aware that many schools have to insist on their own 'basic' science departments and their own 'basic' science research work lest they lose their attractiveness to good scientists, but I suggest that where such duplication exists it represents a failure on the part of the university adequately to recognize the nature of the task of a professional school or to control the transactions between the 'pure' and 'applied' sciences.

FIGURE 18 *Organizational model for the operating systems of a school of professional training*

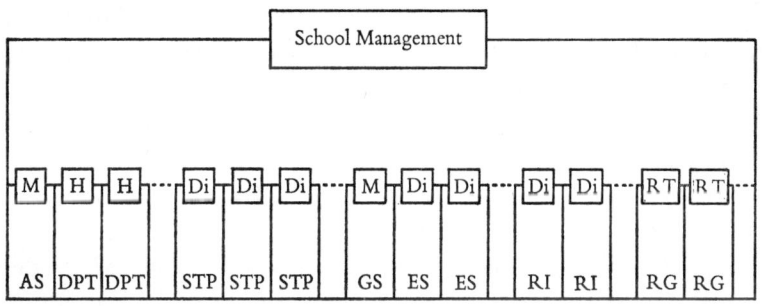

M: Management
H: Head of department
Di: Directorate of service or institute
RT: Research tycoon
AS: Admission system
GS: Graduation system

DPT: Dept of pre-professional training
STP: Service teaching practice
ES: Experimental service
RI: Research institute
RG: Research group

In *Figure 18* I have not shown any control or service functions, or any sentient groups in the managing system. They are likely to be of the same kind as those shown in the model organization of an institution for undergraduate education, and I propose to discuss these again in the next chapter when I consider a model organization for a total university, including schools of professional training. Nor have I shown a tutorial or a supervisory system. Theoretically, at least, postgraduate students should not require a tutorial system such as that I have outlined for undergraduates. Postgraduate students are presumed to be adult. I do not want to suggest for a moment that growth and maturation are not a continuing process, or that adults do not frequently require help in this area, but I am making the assumption that in postgraduate educational institutions there should be no need for a differentiated and institutionalized operating system. In those universities in which colleges are established, postgraduate students frequently remain attached to their college and take part in its 'living' process; they may also retain a close relationship with their undergraduate tutor. Those who change universities on graduation may have a more difficult time.

For them in particular, but also for other postgraduate students, some kind of supervisory system is, I believe, still required. If it incorporates some of the attributes of the tutorial system as well, so much the better. All professional education, whether teaching the theory and practice of a recognized profession or not, suffers perhaps even more than undergraduate education from the increasing array of specialized and diverging branches of knowledge. The problem is particularly acute in medicine and management, to take examples from the recognized and the unrecognized professions. It is no longer possible for a doctor or a manager to be a specialist in every branch of his profession. But both the patient, the *raison d'être* of the doctor, and the enterprise, the *raison d'être* of the manager, are more than a collection of parts, each looked after by a different specialist. Each requires somebody to comprehend the whole. Yet in medicine the generalist already has lower status than the specialist; and in enterprises the general manager is beginning to have to fight an increasing army of specialists for his right to manage.

A supervisory system could help to check fragmentation and diversity in professional education. The same supervisor throughout training could help the student to reconcile the demands of different specializations. Again, however, as in undergraduate education, the system will not achieve an integrative function merely by putting it into the organizational model. It will work effectively only if those responsible for professional education believe in its need; that is, if the culture of the school is congruent with the definition and method of performance of its primary task.

I said earlier that professional training in the real sense had to include practice under supervision. I recognize that this is not yet fully realizable in many professions and quasi-professions. But I believe that more could be done. If business schools, for example, cannot yet make the kinds of relationship with business enterprises that medical schools make with hospitals, they could, nevertheless, use their own organization and management more imaginatively than appears usual. But then, when I hear students of anthropology complaining that their studies appear to have little relevance to contemporary society, I cannot help wondering why anthropology departments themselves should not provide proper areas for anthropological analysis.

Perhaps more pertinently, I deplore, among members of the faculties of professional schools, the growing habit of practising their profession individually, without reference to the institution to which they belong. If the appropriate practice for the members of the faculty of a business school is consultancy, then I am convinced that the school will benefit considerably if the practice is institutionalized and the relationship between school and practice is formalized. Individual practice may be more financially rewarding; it may enrich the individual's teaching and research; but it introduces still another diversification into an already fragmented field.

But the difficulty goes further. I have said that the increase in the number of specialists (and the denigration of the generalist) has led to fragmentation and diversity in professional education. Inevitably, it is also leading to fragmentation and diversity in the professions themselves. I take the medical profession as my example.

The demand, particularly during the past few years, by the people (and government) of the United Kingdom, and elsewhere in the world, for more comprehensive health services is well documented. The demand is for new kinds of service and for more of them. During the same time, the costs of health services have risen rapidly. The combination of demand for more supplies and increased costs is leading to a re-examination of the methods of delivery and of the skills required. The medical profession, which up to now has held a virtual monopoly in the delivery of health services, is having to come to terms with other workers, less highly trained and less expensive, who are taking over some of its functions. Hopefully, these workers are referred to under the general title of the 'allied' health professions. It may be wise for medical schools to consider whether they should not take positive steps towards the integration of the various new professions, lest what are at present the 'allied' professions be forced into trying to become the 'alternative' professions.

An important point is that top medical schools may have a choice: to train a medical elite and leave other schools of lower status to train the auxiliaries, or to redirect both their education and their research to the production of an integrated health-service system. What distinguishes a system of activities from an aggregate is the regulation of the relationships of the activities to each other and of the whole to its environment. Such regulation is likely to be more effective if those who carry out the activities are trained in a common centre, particularly if the training institution itself provides a model of such integration.

Universities may have objections to giving their name to any training that does not lead to graduation. I accept that a university must maintain its standard of scholarship, but I feel nevertheless that if the professional school is to be one of the institutions that relate the university to contemporary society, then it is not appropriate to allow boundaries between sub-systems of the same basic discipline to become impermeable barriers. What may be required is a new, or at least a fresher, concept of the profession. This, I suggest, is more likely to come out of a good school than out of an inferior one.

In effect, should not professional schools become schools of the total professions, instead of just schools of particular parts of them? If new integrated services are to be discovered, and pilot models demonstrated, then innovation and powerful leadership will be required. I suggest that such leadership will be more likely to be followed if the institution in which it is exercised incorporates all the teaching and research activities necessary to design and staff the new services. The argument reinforces the point made at the beginning of this chapter. Professional training is not the same task as undergraduate education or postgraduate research work. It therefore calls for a different kind of organization and different kinds of boundary control. If they are to be able to incorporate advances in knowledge without increasing professional fragmentation, and to respond appropriately to society's demands for services, schools for professional training must have a flexible organization. Moreover, they require sufficient autonomy to enable them to change without having to wait for a major reorganization of the whole university.

CHAPTER 8

A Model Organization for a University

To design an organization for a university that incorporates all the tasks discussed in earlier chapters, I have to reconcile:

(a) the multiplicity of tasks – the discovery and dissemination of knowledge, the provision of opportunities for growth and maturation, the teaching of research methodology, and professional training;

(b) the different levels at which the tasks are performed – undergraduate, postgraduate, post-doctoral, and faculty;

(c) the complexity of discontinuities and continuities in parallel systems – teaching, supervising, and tutorial;

(d) the different kinds of management control required at different boundaries – externally, with the sources of students and faculty, with the local community, and with society; internally, between different task and sentient systems.

It is very tempting to suggest that many different kinds of institution should be established. Each institution could then be given more limited objectives, and some of the complexity arising from having so many different tasks with such indeterminate priorities would be avoided. Indeed, in the affiliate universities of India, and in the undergraduate colleges of America, versions of this kind of differentiation already exist. I would argue, however, just as committees and commissions of inquiry have argued, that, though the tasks of a university are independent of one another to a certain extent, they have such interdependence that, however loosely and flexibly, they should ideally all be performed within the same comprehensive institution.

The reputation of an educational institution – its capacity to attract and hold good faculty and good students, and to maintain high standards – depends ultimately on the quality of its outputs: graduates, postgraduates, professional practitioners, and research findings. I do not suggest that the quality of the outputs should be judged only by academic standards, for other, less measurable, criteria are also relevant. Among them, perhaps the most important is a capacity to take leadership roles in other than academic institutions: government, industry and commerce, the professions, and the social services. But this argument has two clear implications: first that the admission of matriculates into the university, and the crossing of internal boundaries at each subsequent stage – particularly from graduate to postgraduate – must be selective; and, second, that the university must provide opportunities that permit highly creative faculty members to produce their best work. Without such opportunities, the most creative will not join the institution; or, if they join, they will not stay. When they go, they will take others with them. Without the very good, the institution is not likely even to retain the good.

Even so, if organizational chaos is to be avoided, different tasks have to be sharply defined and organizational boundaries precisely drawn. Each specific task requires specific skills, an appropriate organization, and a congruent culture. Discriminations have to be made between:

(a) roles and those who take them;
(b) role competence and personal status;
(c) role and personal relationships;
(d) real and spurious academic freedom.

A comprehensive university carries out so many tasks that few, if any, members of the staff are likely to be competent at many of them. Nor is it likely that all the members of staff engaged in the same task will be equally competent. So much is obvious. But it means that the culture of the whole cannot even pretend to preserve the myth of 'academic freedom' for all. Rather, academic freedom can be granted, and in the appropriate degree, only where it is part of the culture that is congruent with task performance. At the same time, opportunities for multiple-role carrying must be provided. I suggest that the provision of such opportunities under controlled conditions embodies the real flexibility and freedom of an academic career; and that the rules existing in many universities – that every member of the faculty should teach so many hours per week or publish so many research papers per year – are the inflexibilities that represent lack of freedom.

An outline model organization for a university is given in *Figure 19*. To simplify the diagram, only one operating system of each kind has been given: one faculty, one college, one research institute, and so on. It will be seen at once that a professional school is a kind of university within a university, a circumstance that, though organizationally obvious and necessary, appears to give rise to considerable conflict in many universities. Because it has to practise, a school may need its own research institutes, groups, and experimental services. Because, if it is a good school, its research and experimental services must be directed towards problems that are significant to its society, it may appear to be more 'relevant' (to use the current word) than other units of the university. Equally, because it is more immediately 'relevant', it is likely to be denigrated by other units as 'applied', or even as a 'trade' school.

In the managing system I have added an additional service function, and a planning and development function. And because the tasks of faculty and students in a university of the present day are essentially different I have shown a faculty council and a student council, with the possibility of their having some kind of coordinating committee for mutual communication. Other control and service functions will undoubtedly be required. I know too little to be precise about their location, but each has to be examined in relation to what it controls or serves and to be located accordingly. In principle, the smaller a function can be, and the lower it can be located in the system hierarchy, consistent with scientific, economic, and technical viability, the better. Thus a laboratory that serves only one department in one faculty should be located in that department. If another department needs to use the same kind of facility, and there is no good scientific, technological, or economic reason against duplication, then duplication will be most efficient. I should add that the amalgamation of such services for logistic reasons frequently adds enormously to the hidden costs by involving numerous people in endless coordinating committees, with the result that it often makes nonsense of apparently sound economic arguments too.

FIGURE 19 *Model organization for a university*

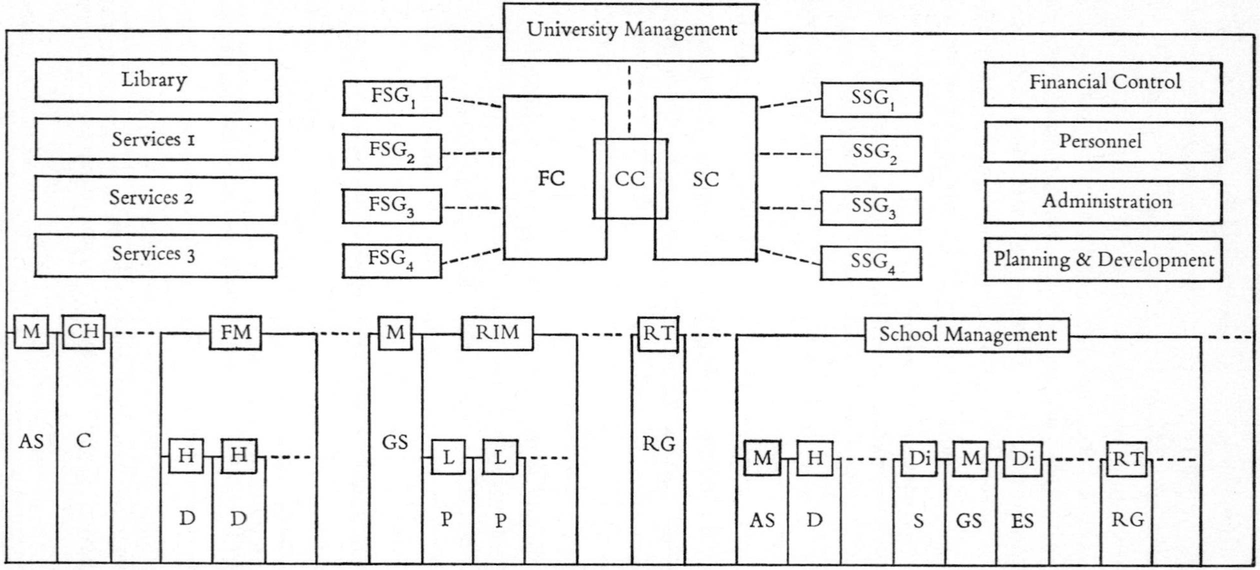

FC: Faculty council
SC: Student council
CC: Coordinating committee
FSG: Faculty sentient group
SSG: Student sentient group
M: Management
CH: College head

FM: Faculty management
RIM: Research institute management
RT: Research tycoon
AS: Admission system
GS: Graduation system
C: College
H: Head of department

D: Department
L: Project & programme leader
P: Project & programme
RG: Research group
Di: Directorate
S: Service
ES: Experimental service

THE PROBLEM OF SIZE

If a university is to be experienced by the members of its faculty and by its students as a coherent whole and as a community, it has to provide a continuous process for them. By this I mean that too many discontinuities, too much coming and going, do not induce stability. It is, of course, healthy for any university if some of its postgraduate students, in both professional training and research work, come from other undergraduate institutions, but it can be disruptive and lead to disintegration if the majority of its postgraduates do not come from its own graduates. The same, with perhaps slightly less emphasis, can be said of the faculty. New blood, introduced at different levels and bringing different experiences, can be stimulating; too much can destroy the identity and special characteristics of the institution.

Consequently, in order to support postgraduate research, research groups, attached research institutes, and professional schools, the undergraduate population has to be large. Hence some form of collegiate system, already described, is essential. Many other solutions have been tried. Some universities have not set up schools for professional training; others have restricted the size of the undergraduate system and have relied on other institutions to provide the majority of their postgraduate intake; still others have severely limited their postgraduate activities, or have had none at all, and have sent their graduates elsewhere for postgraduate training. Others again have just become huge. I believe the last solution to be the worst. The complex activities of a university are difficult enough to manage. Massive size merely compounds the confusion.

Ideally, the smallest university that can offer the whole range of activities, provide for the majority of its own throughput of students from matriculation to doctorate, and recruit a good portion of its faculty from its own alumni, is the most appropriate size. I do not mean that the majority of a university's faculty members should be recruited *directly* from its newly qualified postgraduates. Indeed, I believe that most should have experience elsewhere between doctorate and faculty membership. But I do suggest that it is lack of control over the coming and going that tends to destroy institutional commitment, and hence the building of a viable institutional culture.

Faculty, institute, school, and departmental empire-building may have to be curbed, and this, in turn, may make the university less responsive to the needs of its society. The balance is uneasy; the essential decisions must be based on the answer to the question: For whose benefit does the institution exist?

So far, I have written in terms of models, and have perhaps equated 'model' and 'ideal' too closely. A model, with compromises, has to provide for what is. It is not much use if it provides only for what should be, but is not.

The model organization, such as I have outlined it, calls for selective admission and increasingly ruthless selection at each discontinuity in the process from matriculate to faculty member. That is, the first boundary control must select students in accordance with a definite concept of what the outputs should be; passing from year to year should be reasonably selective; graduation should be highly selective; and only the most promising should be taken into postgraduate education. The model assumes that selection procedures are sufficiently sophisticated to make few mistakes in such a process, which, in the rapidly changing conditions of today, is extremely doubtful. Moreover, it ignores, on the one hand, the increasing number of matriculates demanding higher education; and, on the other, the need, in countries with severe minority problems, to redress the balance of disadvantage by lowering the standards of admission for those whose primary and secondary education has been neglected.

Such constraints may have to be accepted, but let there be no mistake about their being constraints. The influx of more matriculates than universities are designed for, and the lowering of admission standards, lead to overcrowding, poorer teaching, and inadequate research. The present is having to do more than its share to redress the wrongs of the past. Even so, the arguments point inexorably to two courses of action, both of which tend to be ignored: first, to the avoidance of massive size, and hence to the creation of a larger number of smaller universities (with cooperation between them for more specialized academic activities) rather than to the indefinite growth of a few; and, second, to the provision of opportunities for growth and maturation rather than to the continued dominance of discipline-based faculties.

A MODEL ORGANIZATION FOR A UNIVERSITY

Just as I argued that the centralization of control and service functions for logistic reasons could add to the hidden costs of operation by involving so many in coordinating activities, so I feel that the apparent scarcity of resources causes us to make the mistake of imagining that one large campus under centralized control and with centralized services would be less costly than a number of smaller autonomous universities. On paper, the one large campus may appear so; but the costs in terms of alienation of both faculty and students, of bottlenecks in decision-making, and of the struggles of management in trying to manage unmanageable complexities, are surely far greater. As to the provision of opportunities for growth and maturation, I would argue that even where special kinds of institution, for example, technical colleges, are set up (and in most societies some such device is required), they too should provide at least as many opportunities for growth and maturation as for vocational training. Without such provision, the instructional system gets swamped with students, many of whom are so immature and unwilling that they can reduce the best of teachers to frustrated incompetence.

Consideration of the model will not be complete without discussion of what I have called university management and university governance — what they comprise and to whom they report. These I propose to take up in Chapter 10. First, however, I wish to discuss some of the major constraints on task performance.

CHAPTER 9

Some Major Constraints on Task Performance

In Chapter 3, when I was discussing university objectives, I suggested that the basic dilemma in universities today was a conflict of value systems: between the values that appear always to accompany the exploitation of scientific discoveries and technological innovations, and those that give highest priority to the life and wellbeing of individual human beings. In later chapters I have examined the dominant import-conversion-export processes related to the different tasks performed by most universities. As a result, I have built model organizations to fit task performances. At various points during the model-building exercise I have indicated some of the constraints that, in practice, must result in organizational compromise. Now I turn to some of the major constraints that are imposed by the environment. The general ones are political, legal, social, and economic; the more particular are the human, scientific, and technological resources available for performance.

Clearly, the political, legal, social, and economic constraints vary between different countries and within the same country. It is not my purpose to try to analyse these differences. Even if I could, they are changing at such a rate that the analysis would be out of date as soon as it was written. Nevertheless, there are some constraints that I believe to be applicable to most universities in most parts of the world. Some are real and unavoidable, others – and it is on these that I want to concentrate – it is within the power of universities to modify if not to remove entirely. I propose to treat them under the following subheadings: participation in decision-making, the dependent culture of the educational process, tenure, the university and its society, the explosion of knowledge, the sophisticated demands of society, the decline in religious belief, and, finally, standards of scholarship.

PARTICIPATION IN DECISION-MAKING

I choose this subheading because it appears to have become the slogan of the students (and the junior members of the faculty) in many universities, and, like so many slogans, it is used without adequate attention to what it means. 'No person has the right to make decisions that affect the lives of others' is a common statement in student newspapers. In Chapter 6, when discussing the managing system of a model organization for an institution for undergraduate education, I said that I believed that both faculty and students, as the members of the university community, should have the opportunity to make their voices heard in the formation of university policy. I deplored, however, the rush to constitution-building, demands for votes, and wrangles about procedures. Nevertheless, I accept that any institution in a democratic society has to come to terms with the demand of its members to 'participate' in the decisions that affect them. Academic institutions, in particular, have always been built on, and for the most part have practised, this principle. But, in recent years, even they have been finding that there have been rather more 'participants' than their structures and cultures have been able to accommodate – participants who have insisted, sometimes with violence, on their rights to a voice not only in the formation of policy but in its implementation as well.

Some of the difficulties experienced by many universities seem to me to be conceptual: confusion, for example, between the democratic processes of policy formulation and the executive processes of implementation. In a political democracy, parties or individuals formulate policies. A sophisticated electorate then decides which is the best policy and whether its advocates can govern, and votes accordingly. If the elected do not govern in accordance with the policy they have announced, they are removed. At least, that is the theory, and it is no condemnation of the philosophy that there so often seems to be little relationship between the policies advocated before elections and what is implemented after them. In the same way, a working group may participate in policy-making, but unless it defines roles and role relationships, and delegates specific authority for implementation to some roles, little is likely to be accomplished. Some of the consequences of confusion between policy-making and implementation can be disastrous: for instance, that every decision has to be referred to democratic procedures, or that no decision can be taken unless a specific person makes it. Both destroy democracy: the former by futility, the latter by dictatorship.

Much of the discussion I hear about the rights of faculty and students to participate in decision-making seems to me to beg the question of the delegation, upwards and downwards, of responsibility and authority for implementation. Of course, implementation nearly always involves interpretation, and interpretation can itself frequently make policy and establish precedent. But, in the long run, a working group that will not tolerate interpretation and implementation by those to whom leadership and executive roles have been assigned destroys its own leaders and renders itself impotent.

It is also unfortunately true that innovation and change seldom appear to result from democratic processes. Innovation and change occur when creative men and women exercise leadership. Sometimes they are followed by a majority and change is easy; sometimes they are followed only by a minority, or by no one at all, and then change occurs only if they are prepared to fight for what they believe in, and are able to win.

In most universities the faculty is involved in the policy-making and decision-making process. In some, it is the whole faculty; in others, the tenured members; in others again, senior faculty or those holding specific offices, such as deans and heads of departments. They are formed into senates or councils, on which outsiders may or may not sit. But in almost every university of which I have any knowledge such bodies are large, cumbersome, and for the most part ineffective. They are too large for free discussion; and they are not, like their government equivalents, divided into parties upon whose support the advocates of certain policies can depend. At best, they can act only as a check on those responsible for management.

Now a working group, whatever its size, must make a continuous evaluation of its task performance, and of the contributions of its individual members to that performance. It must have mechanisms to support those who perform effectively, and to discriminate against those who fail. Adequate safeguards, however, are not to be found in the introduction of checks and balances so numerous that stagnation is almost inevitable, or of built-in rules and procedures so detailed that leadership is forever having to convene meetings that are frequently dull and are a waste of expensive time. The best safeguards are effective means of removing from office those who do not match the standards required.

I feel certain that when universities were much smaller, and their policy-making bodies were small, compact, working groups, the latter probably provided both a salutary check on over-ambitious leaders and a constructive support for innovation and change. But such bodies have grown large, too large even for easy discussion. I can only suggest that they should initiate their own dissolution, and be replaced by one or more of the sentient groups outlined in Chapters 6 and 8. Such groups would be more consistent with the need for all groups to be involved in policy formation, and, at the same time, would make it possible for faculty members to make constructive contributions rather than merely endorse or veto decisons of the management.

Much the same kind of consideration needs to be given, I feel, to the role of heads of departments. In the first place, are they chairmen of their faculty meetings, or are they directors? If they are chairmen, then members of their departments will have the major say in their appointment and removal; if they are directors, then they will be appointed by a higher authority. The ambiguity, I believe, serves to avoid some difficult questions about their responsibility and authority; and hence about what is expected of them. But, however they are appointed, their authority can be only as great or as little as the structure and culture allow. I feel that what is frequently an ambiguous status represents a built-in invitation to them either to succumb to enervating administrative routine or to use personal manipulation or truculence to get their own way. Organizationally, they are inhibited by the lack of definition of sanction for their management; culturally, they are inhibited by the pervading climate of participation in every decision-making process.

I have discussed earlier the importance I attach to institutional as well as to individual models of behaviour in educational institutions. It is, perhaps, hardly to be wondered at that junior members of the faculty and students in many universities are growing impatient and are, on the one hand, trying to invent new models of their own, and, on the other, exploiting the existing uncertainties to embarrass leadership. Although as soon as they achieve the role of 'participants in decision-making' they find themselves in the same bind, this does not stop them from clamouring for their rights. Indeed, the present situation encourages irresponsible revolutionary activity.

I believe, however, that the difficulties go deeper. Because the organization inhibits leadership, the only people who can succeed are those who are so tough and insensitive that they do not mind riding rough-shod over others' feelings, or so persuasive and politically devious that they are able to exploit the existing confusion. I exaggerate and oversimplify to make the point. But it does seem that task-oriented, logical, decisive, yet sensitive, leadership has a far harder time than the institution, the faculty, or the students, deserve. And management that does set out to define and control boundaries, and to administer effectively, tends to be denigrated and to be accused of serving some political power group or other.

The real problem about participation in decision-making is that it allows a working group to avoid what are probably its most painful decisions – the decisions that discriminate between its members on grounds of competence. Or, rather, it allows the group to avoid open discussion of these decisions and forces their covert implementation – because the discriminations are made and the decisions are implemented, otherwise standards could not be maintained. The discriminations and decisions are made, then, not by the group as a group, but by those who exercise personal power rather than role authority. Two consequences follow: first, decisions about task performance become overlaid by personal conflicts; and, second, and more importantly, a working group that claims the authority to participate in decision-making is shown to have abdicated in the face of having to make a painful decision. The former is not uncommon: most working groups find it difficult to separate role and personal relationships. The latter is common enough too, but it is particularly disastrous in an institution that provides, or should provide, a model of engaging 'vigorously and fearlessly in the pursuit of truth'.

THE DEPENDENT CULTURE OF THE EDUCATIONAL PROCESS

In my discussion of professional training in Chapter 7, I drew attention to the dependent culture inherent in those professions that provide services to society. I also considered the problem of over-determined identification between teacher and taught arising from the apprenticeship nature of much of the practical training, and the consequent reality-testing that faculty practice involved. In this section, I wish to suggest that any educational process, whether at primary, secondary, or higher level, requires the development of a dependent culture. I go further and suggest that it is the breakdown of the dependent culture that is at least contributing to the apparent irrationality of many of today's conflicts between faculty and students.

The process of education assumes that somebody (in this context, the faculty) knows something that is of value to others (the students). As a minimum, the faculty is expected to provide an environment in which students can learn. Students are thus dependent on the faculty. But the faculty, in turn, depends on students. Empty classes, unattended supervisions, do no good to the reputation of a teacher. Mutual dependency, even when sophisticated, can hardly help but generate some hostility whenever mistakes are made or expectations are unfulfilled (as is bound to happen sometimes in any human situation). Because of the dependency, however, the hostility is often denied or suppressed; and it is the denial or suppression that leads to the greatest danger, since the dependent leader is tempted to believe in his putative omniscience or omnipotence. Alternatively, the hostility may lead to open conflict, but, because some of its causes are denied, the conflict itself becomes irrational. The faculty tends to impose arbitrary rules on students about class attendance and extra-curricular behaviour. Students, in turn, claim the right to redesign curricula and have all-elective courses with no compulsory attendance, and then object to being examined and graded on what they have or have not learned.

Furthermore, junior members of the faculty often depend on their senior colleagues for their future careers, and senior members of the faculty depend on their ability to attract and hold brilliant juniors. Again, the inherent hostility arising from the mutual dependency is frequently denied or suppressed; and members of the junior faculty go into collusion with the protesting and rioting students to destroy the establishment, or they take open sides with the students and usually suffer the same fate – suspension or dismissal. And many faculty members, both senior and junior, still holding to their ideal of a university as a community of scholars who learn from each other and enrich the lives of mankind with their pursuit of knowledge, are bewildered by what is happening to them. In their bewilderment they become frustrated, and the more frustrated they become, the more they feel they are subject to erratic and arbitrary external controls, and the more they claim 'freedom' from any internal control. They demand the right to teach what they like, irrespective of the coherence or consistency of courses; to choose their own research projects, irrespective of their relevance to contemporary problems (even in the long term); to maintain an egalitarian culture, irrespective of competence; and to be granted permanent tenure whatever their ability.

An unsophisticated dependent culture is particularly dangerous at a time of change. It permits members of the faculty individually to insist that change is essential, and collectively to oppose any change proposed. It makes the role of leadership well-nigh intolerable.

TENURE

Historically, I believe that 'tenure' was granted to the faculties of academic institutions to protect them first from religious, and later from political, persecution. But it seems now that in many universities it is being used less as a means of protecting intellectual freedom than as a weapon in the competition for promotion and as a passport to positions of power. At least this is so in universities in which tenure is synonymous with office-holding. Tenure as a protection against persecution and as a guarantee of job security may still, unfortunately, be necessary. My doubt is whether, in an age of such rapid change, it should also carry with it the automatic right of membership of a 'governing body'. Where it confers this right, there is a danger that tenure will act as a built-in obstacle to change: innovation, particularly in institution-building to deal with modern conditions, can only too easily be sacrificed to tradition and precedent. Tradition may be important and should perhaps be preserved, but never at the expense of what should now be added, and certainly not at the expense of the destruction of innovative leadership.

What is required, it seems, is to make a sharp distinction between two elements of job security: the right to a livelihood and the right to a position. If the only chair in a particular discipline is occupied by somebody who, by reason of age or failing capacities, can no longer fill it adequately, then, in the interests of the institution, its faculty, and its students, he should be removed. But if no socially acceptable mechanism exists for removing him from the post without depriving him of his livelihood, then either he remains in it, and those who could fill it leave the institution, or underground campaigns to get him out are resorted to – life has to be made so uncomfortable that he will leave.

This brings me back to the problem of a working group's capacity to tolerate discrimination among its own members. Without discrimination a vicious circle is set up: those who suspect that their competence is not highly regarded by their colleagues are forced into over-determined self-defence, which, in turn, reduces the regard still further, and increases the defensive manoeuvres. In no time at all, somebody who is quite competent is believed by his colleagues, and often by himself, to be incompetent. Of course, high standards have to be maintained, but I believe that they are better maintained when they are discussed in concrete reality as well as in abstract principle.

I do not wish in any way to minimize the difficulties. It is extraordinarily, and often impossibly, painful to discuss individual performance in a group; it is still very painful, but not impossible, in a pair. To allow such paired discussion, however, a working group has to be prepared to entrust its authority and responsibility to one of its members, in effect to its leader. The group can always withdraw its delegation if it does not like what is being done. Perhaps this is the greatest fear of all: that authority once entrusted cannot be withdrawn. But this, to me, is the denial of individual responsibility, without which democracy cannot survive.

To maintain job security without pre-empting office-holding may require the creation of sinecures; but this may be a small price to pay if it revitalizes university management.

THE UNIVERSITY AND ITS SOCIETY

I have already emphasized that a university, in the present day, is unlikely to be able to isolate itself from its society. No university, so far as I know, has sufficient resources of its own to maintain itself or can obtain a sufficient income from fees alone. The private foundations have to receive public support in one form or another, in grants for students, research, buildings, or equipment. Because they use public funds, universities have to respond to public needs. But this does not mean that they have to respond to every need, or that they have to abandon entirely their tradition of scholarship in the interests of immediate contemporary events. Universities are, or should be, enduring institutions transmitting more than the short-term values of their society. Moreover, universities are related not only to their own societies but to the world of knowledge, to their counterparts in other societies. Local pressure for local needs, and local constraints, may have to be accepted, but if they dominate a university, that university is unlikely to endure even as a national, let alone an international, institution. And in terms of the quality of its outputs, I believe this to be true whether the university is a private, local, state, or national institution.

The important point is that a university has multiple tasks to perform, which are different from the tasks of other institutions in society. It requires, therefore, its own institutional form and its own organization, and these will be different from those of other institutions and of society itself. The *Report of the committee on relations with junior members*[1] is quite explicit:

'In our view, no theory of legal or political rights for the conduct of a society as a whole, not even democratic theory, is transferable to these distinctly academic activities (research and teaching). Since there are these distinctive purposes to be pursued, it is, we believe, plain that teachers equipped by skill, knowledge and experience, training and continuing professional association with a university should have final authority as to the manner in which they are pursued.'

Another point is that unless a university makes up its mind what it

[1] See H. L. A. Hart (1969). London: Oxford University Press.

can do best, and formulates and pursues its policy accordingly, it is unlikely to command the loyalty of its faculty to itself as an institution. One disastrous consequence of the present turmoil and disorganization in universities generally is that good faculty members, loyal to scholarship, appear to spend a great deal of their time moving from job to job, trying to find the peace to do what they can do. But this very movement produces a vicious circle: it disturbs the rhythm of work, and gives too little time to build viable units; and the stablility and continuity that do exist come from those who are not good enough to move. I exaggerate, of course, but I do so to make the point, to which I shall have to address myself in the chapter on university governance, that 'academic scholarship' is not an institution in the sense that it can ever be more than an aggregate of scholars. What is surely needed today is institutions with declared policies that can command the support, drive, and abilities of both their faculties and their students.

THE EXPLOSION OF KNOWLEDGE

I have already discussed under other headings the effects on teaching and research of the explosion of knowledge in the sciences. Owing to the number and diversity of specializations, and the status accorded to the specialist as against the generalist, there has been a tendency to ignore the student as a person. Students resent, consciously or unconsciously, being treated as a collection of parts at the disposal of academic faculties. But it is mainly the rapid increase in knowledge and technology in other fields that I am thinking of here, in particular, in communications and data-processing.

The development and application of computers is still a comparatively young technology. It is easy to speculate that in the next decade or generation it will revolutionize most of the sciences and probably some of the arts as well. It is far harder to accept – at least for the older generation – that what it may do is so to change their fields that the skills that are highly valued today, or were yesterday, may be much less regarded or rewarded in the comparatively near future. Mathematics, systems analysis, and their applications to computer technology, belong to a young man's world. We of the older generation may understand the principles, and even many of the practices, of computer technology. But I fear we may not always be able to cope with all the data that are now, or will be, put at our disposal; or, rather, we may not always appreciate the significance of what the data do or do not tell us. The wisdom born of long, and often painfully acquired, experience, on which our judgements used to be based, is no longer sufficient. Moreover, when we had to make judgements with little hard data, perhaps we could be forgiven, and forgive ourselves, for the mistakes we made.

At the same time, the remarkably rapid strides in communication technology not only call into question traditional teaching and research methods, but expose senior faculty (among many other previously privileged classes) to far more professional and public scrutiny than they have ever had to endure in the past. It is easy for the conservative to sneer at the 'television dons', to question their motives for popularizing their subjects and themselves, but I fear they are only a portent of what is in store. The time when a member of a faculty could do his one piece of research, and then live out his academic career on a standard series of lectures, has gone. Rightly so, perhaps, but it does not necessarily reconcile some members of university faculties to the changes that are happening around them.

THE SOPHISTICATED DEMANDS OF SOCIETY

The increasing sophistication of society, which is also, in part, a result of the development of communication technology, is leading to new demands on universities. Society now demands attention to its contemporary problems, and a much quicker pay-off for its investments. This has already had two predictable consequences: a reduction in the uniqueness of university education, and the introduction of some of the characteristics of mass production into what was reserved for the elite. And mass production in higher education has, as in other fields, lowered quality and restricted innovation. In other words, the gap between the elite universities and the normal run of higher education is likely to grow rather than decrease. At least it will grow unless the elite universities themselves take a lead in the modifications – a lead that many scholars feel would be a betrayal of much of what they stand for.

In a sense, the scholars who feel this way are right. It seems to me that universities are being asked to take perhaps too great a part in solving a perennial problem of civilized society – what it is now fashionable to call the problem of the 'generation gap'. There is no doubt that the problem exists, but it always has. Socrates had some trenchant things to say about 'rebellious youth'; and many other writers before and since have deplored youth's destructive attacks on 'the establishment'. And it is not so many years ago, historically speaking, that the army had to be called in to quell an uprising by the pupils of an English public school. The question is why the problem takes its contemporary form, and why it appears to be so prevalent in universities – the one place where, by tradition, faculty and students form a community.

One reason is that opportunities for adventure, for experiment, for discovering something new, are more limited than they were. There are no longer new territories to be discovered, new heights to be climbed, or 'backward' peoples to be introduced to the 'benefits' of civilization; or, at least, none that is available to the ordinary youth of today. Modern technology has made adventure and experiment too costly. When Amundsen and Scott went to the South Pole it was high adventure; nobody had been there before; the major qualifications for getting there were more physical than intellectual. Today, modern technology maintains permanent settlements in the Antarctic; the qualifications required are largely scientific; the problem is not so much courage and endurance as the disposal of garbage in a frozen landscape. The new territories are the moon, the planets, and the universe. Magnificent though achievements in such fields are, and will be, only a few, a very few, of today's youth can hope to participate in them. And the very achievements themselves draw increasing attention to the unsolved human and social problems on earth.

More generally, I suggest that the real problem of the generation gap is to find constructive and socially acceptable outlets for youthful aggression – an essential process of growth and maturation. Armed warfare, even if it can be justified ideologically, is too universally destructive to be humanly acceptable. Other kinds of warfare – on poverty, disease, and other human ills – seldom appear to have the same satisfying appeal; probably because by their very nature they are peaceful in intent. But outlets have to be found, and if socially acceptable ones cannot be found, unacceptable ones will be. Increasingly vicious economic and social competition is one such outlet; street gangs among urban youth, football crowds, 'mods and rockers', and crime are other outlets. Among university students, the intellectual elite of their societies, it does not seem unreasonable to direct aggression against the social and political institutions that perpetuate a self-defeating system; or that universities, as privileged institutions of that system, should so frequently be the targets of attack.

THE DECLINE IN RELIGIOUS BELIEF

When I turn to the decline of religious belief I find myself on less certain ground. There seems little doubt, however, that since the first world war, and especially since the second, there has been a noticeable decline in man's belief that the world's problems will be solved by prayer – a decline that can be attributed both to disillusionment with war itself and to increasing scientific knowledge, which challenges many religious tenets. Nevertheless, since civilization began, man has used religion in its various forms as a means of controlling one of the most frightening boundaries he has to cross – from life to death. The decline in religious belief has not led to an equivalent mitigation of this fear. Indeed, since modern knowledge appears only to increase the possibilities of violent death, some faith, some belief, is desperately needed to replace the hope that has been lost.

The prevalent belief is that if only enough money is spent any problem can be solved. I think it is fair to speculate that the intellectual elite of the universities, particularly in the humanities and perhaps in the social sciences, are being asked to produce some answers, and quickly. The less attention they pay to contemporary problems and the further they retire into their scholarly but detached ivory towers, the more hatred they arouse and the more they will be attacked.

STANDARDS OF SCHOLARSHIP

I take for granted that any university has to be jealous of its reputation, and hence of the quality of its outputs. This means that the performance of both its faculty and its students must match criteria that will be acceptable not only to itself but to the academic world. One difficulty, which I have already mentioned in the chapter on university research, is that, whereas in the so-called natural sciences the criteria for judgement of performance are established and generally recognized, there are no such accepted criteria for measuring the outputs of the clinical or applied sciences. Perhaps a greater difficulty still is that there were such recognized criteria for the judgement of scholarship in the humanities, but that was before philosophers were expected to provide answers to pressing social problems.

I have already made my own prejudices clear, and will not labour the point. But I cannot forbear one more quotation from the report of the President of Yale University for 1967-68:

> 'Practical problems can be just as intellectually rigorous, just as challenging to intellectual ingenuity as the solving of more theoretical puzzles or the search for a more abstract truth. Clinical teaching and research need not genuflect before the pure medical scientist. Action oriented legal scholarship and teaching can be at least as rigorous and stimulating as the model building of the "pure" social scientist.'

I would go further and suggest that intellectual rigour and ingenuity have to be all the greater when they are applied to the messy, complex, multiple variables of community life. We cannot afford slipshod thinking, or balking at emotional fences. The thinking has to be ruthless; its application insightful, understanding, and compassionate.

CHAPTER 10

University Governance

In Chapter 8 I outlined a model organization for a comprehensive university, encompassing undergraduate and postgraduate education; research departments, institutes, and groups; and schools for professional training. In the research departments, graduates could be taught research techniques and earn higher degrees; and in the research institutes and groups, problems could be solved and creative research workers could do their own work. In the schools, graduates could be given training in their chosen profession and, through research institutes and groups, the profession could be enlarged and enriched by new discoveries and new methods of practice. The model makes provision for members of the faculty to take multiple roles in different systems of activity and to belong to sentient groups, so that they have several roles and several routes through which they can make their voice heard. In so doing, however, it also provides almost endless opportunites for the confusion of task-system boundaries and of the authorities and responsibilities attached to different roles. I suggested that to maintain the definition of these boundaries would require sophisticated behaviour on the part of members of the faculty. I suggested, further, that university management, and, by implication, college, faculty, institute, and school managements, would have to act with authority in order to reinforce appropriate forms of behaviour and to inhibit inappropriate forms.

What must now be added is that, in conditions of change, which call for imagination and innovation, university management must provide imaginative, innovative, and adaptive leadership as well. And if university management is to be supported, the management of its sub-institutions must also provide imaginative, innovative, and adaptive leadership. A university cannot afford to let its management degenerate into an arid administrative function.

Many committees and commissions have insisted that, if they are

UNIVERSITY GOVERNANCE

to discharge their function adequately, universities must have autonomy. They must be free from interference. Whatever external bodies and individuals – in the form of governments, university grants committees, chancellors, corporations, visitors, and so on – may have to do with the control and inspection of universities, one thing is clear: that once university management has been appointed to carry out a task and has been given and accepted its terms of reference, it must be allowed to do the job – to formulate and implement policies that are in accordance with its statutes. That is, university management must have the responsibility and authority to control transactions with its environment. This means, then, that its administrative procedures cannot be laid down by any external authority, particularly by one that imposes procedures designed for a different purpose, for example, government. Nor can university staff be chosen, or their conditions of service laid down, by other than university management.

In practice, some compromises may, of course, be necessary to satisfy social, political, legal, and economic constraints. But every such compromise must be recognized as a vote of no confidence in university management. In addition to reducing the responsibility and authority of management, constraint and compromise weaken its capacity for leadership. Too many constraints inevitably destroy leadership.

THE ROLE OF VICE-CHANCELLOR

And that brings me to the question of who should manage. The Robbins Report[1] on Higher Education in the United Kingdom stated:

'No other enterprise would impose on its chairman the variety and burden of work that a modern university requires of its Vice-Chancellor.'

It may be that the traditional role of vice-chancellor, or president, is no longer viable in universities in today's conditions. The Model Act in India says:

'He is at once a member of the governing body and the chairman

[1] Ministry of Education, 1963, *Report of the Committee on Higher Education, 1961–63* (Chairman: Lord Robbins) (Cmnd. 2154). London: H.M.S.O.

of the main academic councils. He must represent his institution in all formal and informal relations with the University Grants Committee; he must be present at meetings of the Committee of Vice-Chancellors and Principals; he must keep in touch with potential benefactors, and he must be aware of developments in the various branches of learning.'

'(He) is by far the most important functionary in a university, not only on the administrative side, but also for securing the right atmosphere for the teachers and students to do their work effectively and in the right spirit.'

It is possible that a strong and very able man could fill all these roles, provided he was not appointed for a fixed short term, was allowed to appoint his own staff, and was left free from interference. But the fulfilment of these conditions would require, as well as a remarkable man, such a change in the political and cultural patterns surrounding university management that it hardly seems practical to persevere with such hopes.

It may be worth while to think of a new organizational concept for university management: not a vice-chancellor, or a president, but a vice-chancellorate, or a presidency, an office that could be filled by more than one man. Two, three, four, or five men or women could probably satisfy the multiple demands of the office and defend the university against interference more effectively than one could. The essential point is that once they were appointed, it would be their responsibility to decide how to sort out their duties and how to manage their relationships. They would be collectively responsible for what the office said and did. It would be unlike the present situation of a vice-chancellor and pro-vice-chancellor, or of a president and vice-presidents or provosts, in which ultimately the full burden of responsibility and authority rests on one man or woman.

The present-day spectacle of so many vice-chancellors and presidents in serious trouble (and of many vacancies that are difficult to fill) does not mean that they are all incompetent leaders, managers, or administrators, but that the tasks they are expected to perform are becoming impossible. To me it is also evidence of outdated organization, organization that has not been adequately studied. And since

UNIVERSITY GOVERNANCE

universities have as their objectives the discovery and dissemination of knowledge, it does not seem unreasonable to expect them to attempt an understanding of their own complexities, and to experiment with their own management.

GOVERNANCE

There still remain two questions: What should the vice-chancellorate control, and to what body should it report? Practice varies widely, from that at the older universities where the vice-chancellor is appointed for a very short period, has little real authority, and reports to a senate of senior faculty, to that in some private universities where the ultimate power lies with a self-perpetuating group of trustees, and the vice-chancellor on their behalf controls all university resources. In some universities the final authority is the government, local or national, that provides the resources; in others, there appears to be no one final authority, but multiple authorities, all of which have to be satisfied.

If a university is to have autonomy in the way it conducts its affairs, then its policy-making body has to be itself; and I have already suggested how to ensure that the members of the university community, both faculty and students, contribute to policy formation. Is this enough? Should the community appoint its own vice-chancellorate? For all the reasons I have given – the use of public resources; the demands of society for the solution, or at least for contributions to the solution, of contemporary problems; and, above all, the tendency of academic institutions to become closed systems – it is my belief that some external authority is required. But I do not think that such an authority can dictate policy or methods of implementation.

It should act as a trustee body for society. It would be the trustees' responsibility to ensure that the university worked in accordance with its statutes, to modify those statutes as required by changing conditions, and, after taking advice, including advice from the university community, to appoint the vice-chancellorate, or other form of management. The trustees would also, of course, have to have the authority to change the management.

When I come to the question of the appropriate composition of such a trustee body, I can only emphasize once again that a university has a number of tasks to perform on behalf of society. It follows that the trustees should be those who are best qualified to judge whether university management is discharging its leadership and management functions satisfactorily. Ideally, an individual should be appointed a trustee because he has demonstrated a capacity to make shrewd judgements about those to whom he entrusts management and policy-making decisions. He may be a politician, an industrialist, an educator; he may, indeed, be a member of the university staff; but he should not sit to represent any kind of constituency. Representation, as such, has no place in trusteeship.

Lest it be thought that I am recommending an authoritarian structure and management, may I stress that, wherever the final authority lies, ultimate power in a university must always reside in the community. A faculty, by withdrawing its support from university management, can always render that management impotent; and students all over the world have demonstrated that, by withdrawing their studentship, they can render the faculty impotent. But if faculty and students are going to exercise such rights, let them do so with responsibility; otherwise they will destroy not only the university but the democratic basis on which it is built.

In a society in which belief in democratic government, and in equal opportunities for all, irrespective of race or religion, is firmly held, discrimination is always regarded with grave suspicion. It is only too easy for the incompetent to believe, and to make out a case, that discrimination against them on the grounds of their incompetence is motivated by political, racial, or religious attitudes. Similarly, it is only too easy for political, racial, and religious groups to demand equal shares in appointments and privileges, irrespective of the competence of their members. Above all, it is easier for authority to define paper qualifications and to determine conditions for whole classes than to make judgements about individuals and to act on those judgements. Effective task performance demands that judgements be made about the quality of the contributions of members of task systems, and that the judgements be acted on. No institution, whatever its organizational structure, can overlook this demand without detriment to task performance, and, in the long run, distortion of task definition.

CHAPTER 11

Conclusion

Throughout this short book, I have tried to suggest that many of the current difficulties in universities do not arise from the incompetence and indifference of their faculties, or from the intemperance and ill will of their students. I have argued that many of them arise from inadequate recognition of the contradictory demands made on universities by their societies. I have suggested that these contradictions result in confused task definition and motivated disorganization. I have to recognize, however, that because the conflicts have been prolonged, and numerous committees and commissions have failed to bring about much change, the problems are now deep-seated and perplexing. Many members of university faculties who were previously competent and enthusiastic have, through frustration and disillusionment, become incompetent and indifferent. And many students who were temperate and reasonable have become intemperate and revolutionary.

So many compromises have already been made, and so many of them have been incorporated into university constitutions, organizations, and practices, that there is little chance of reform or change by legislative action, by decree or regulation imposed from outside. In reality, some compromise is always necessary between organizations for different tasks, between task and sentient systems, and between the organization of the whole and the organizations of its various parts. The problem in many universities today is that many of the compromises have become so hallowed by tradition that it is almost impossible to recognize the difference between them and organizational principles. In other words, changes in constitution or in organization are useless by themselves. There is no purely organizational solution to motivated disorganization while the motives that underlie the disorganization remain unchanged. Some solutions, and the most difficult to implement, can only be behavioural.

If the definitions of the tasks implicit in the statement of university objectives can be agreed, and if the consequences of effective task performance can be accepted, then an analysis such as I have attempted may reduce the threat of change, at least sufficiently to permit experimental reorganization. Nevertheless, whatever is done, it has to be recognized that the interdependence of tasks, as well as the tasks themselves, will remain complex. Complex tasks require a complex institution with a complex organization. I do not believe that a simple solution exists. Nor do I believe that in a complex organization there is often a simple correlation between cause and effect. Above all, I do not think that any one modification, or series of modifications, will suffice to bring about adequate change in either university structure or university culture. Many of the changes, both explicit and implicit, that arise from this analysis are, like the multiple tasks of a university, interdependent: any one change is dependent on others.

Moreover, the changes cannot be made overnight. Even willing change will take time. This means that the leadership that attempts change must be prepared to tolerate the anxiety that is inevitably entailed in waiting for results; anxiety that will be aggravated by doubts about the changes initiated, and, more painfully, by opposition from those whose vested and traditional interests are being eroded. And in academic circles such opposition is most dangerous when it is reasonable and well argued rather than emotional and overtly hostile.

In the introduction I wrote that I approached the problems of change in universities as though there were a green-field site, without buildings, faculty, students, or traditions. I accepted that this was an unachievable ideal. But what may be possible is a pilot experiment in a university whose governance and management want to innovate and to change. Its existing organization could be compared with the model, and the reasons for disparities between them could be investigated. Agreed change in the direction of the model might then be made. The effects of these changes could be examined, and further changes could be made in the direction of the original model, or of a model modified as a result of the first experiment. It might then be possible to decide whether there is any reality in my argument that the more rigorous definition of the boundaries of task

CONCLUSION

and sentient systems in such a complex institution as a modern university would permit transactions, externally with the environment and internally between the parts, to be controlled in the interests of more effective task performance.

This last paragraph observes the difficulties of the process. Even with consensus about the definitions of university tasks and with acceptance of the consequences of reorganization, it might still be very hard to reach agreement about the first experimental changes; at least, a sufficient level of agreement to ensure that sabotage would not invalidate experimental results (and the sabotage would not all be conscious). Throughout the book I have indeed argued that there is in the majority of universities massive unconscious agreement to maintain organizational confusion in order to avoid recognition of the conflict of cultural values. Only if the authorities that govern universities will first agree to long-term experiment does there seem much chance of reaching agreement at other levels. And agreement by the governing authorities implies that most of them would have to accept a reduction of their power; and some of them, at least, might have to be prepared to liquidate themselves.

Index

'academic freedom', 29, 82
'academic scholarship', 97
action research, 62
activity systems, see under system(s)
administration, 67, 103
admission, 82, 86
affiliate universities, 81
aggregate of activities, 8, 80
aggression, outlets for, 99, 100
Allahabad, University of, 20
America, see United States
Amundsen, R., 99
anthropology, 79
applied sciences, 101
  see also, research, applied
apprenticeship, 74, 75, 93
architecture, 73, 75
arts, the, 75
authorities and responsibilities
  delegation of, 90
  of heads of departments, 91
  identification of, 5
  of leadership, 57
  of a profession, 73
  of role, 64, 92, 102
  of a teacher, 46
  of a tutor, 53, 61
  of university management, 103, 104
  of working groups, 95
autonomy
  in professional schools, 80
  in research units, 29, 33, 34
  in a university, 103, 104

'basic-science' departments, 39, 77

behaviour
  adult models of, 53, 57, 62, 65, 70, 91
  of faculty members, 42, 102
  institutional models of, 91
  organizational models of, 70
  professional standards of, 73
  sophisticated, 66, 102
  of students, 53, 59
  values underlying, 52
behavioural solutions, 107
biological sciences, 35, 36, 72
boundaries
  of activity systems, 4, 5, 12
  confusion of, 64, 102
  control of, 5, 8–10, 11, 30, 42, 44, 80, 81, 86, 92
  crossing of, 82
  definition of, 46–7, 92, 102, 108
  departmental, 35
  of an enterprise, 17
  impermeable, 40, 80
  organizational, 12, 68, 82
  sentient-system, 11, 12, 13
  subject, 42
  task-system, 11, 17, 18, 19, 39, 64, 102
  transactions across, 8, 46, 103, 109

Cambridge, University of, 66
change, see innovation and change
chaos, definition of, 18
classics, 49
closed system, university as, 4
clubs, 57
colleges, 60, 66, 78
collegiate system, 66, 67, 85

111

collusion, 61, 94
commitment, 29, 31, 52, 85
committees, 65
communication
   between academic disciplines, 21
   between faculty and management, 3
   between faculty and students, 2
   formal systems of, 13
   technology, 97, 98
competitiveness, 23
compromise, 12, 47, 103, 107
computer technology, 97, 98
conflict
   of cultural values, 22, 109
   personal, 92
   of systems, 13
constitution-building, 67, 89
constraints, 12, 13, 86, 103
consultancy, 79
control
   departmental, 42
   faculty, 42
   financial, 31, 67, 96
   mechanisms, 46
   professional, 27
   of source of data, 27, 39
   uncertainty of, 19
control and service functions
   centralization of, 83, 87
   definition of, 11
   in an enterprise, 9
   of institutional management, 66, 67
   in model university organization, 83
   of research-programme management, 34
   of research-unit management, 31, 37
   of sentient groups, 68
conversion activities, 7
conversion processes
   in an educational institution, 41
   in an enterprise, 7-8, 9, 11, 12
   in a problem-centred research unit, 30
   in a research institute, 28
   in undergraduate education, 58
   in a university, 46, 52, 88
conversion systems, *see under* system(s)
creative workers, 36, 37, 71, 82
creativity, 67, 90
curricula, 74, 93
culture
   congruent, 51, 78, 82
   dependent, 88, 93-4
   institutional, 85
   permissive, 51

data-processing, 67, 97
decision-making
   in growth and maturation, 51-2
   investment function of, 37, 40
   machinery of, 23
   participation in, 61, 87, 88, 89-92
degrees, 41, 56, 71
departmental boundaries, 35
departmental control, 42
departmental heads, 46, 47, 91
departmental management, 35
departments, 60, 62, 66
   discipline-based, 35, 36, 37, 39, 64, 66, 71, 73, 76, 86
dependent culture, *see under* culture
diplomas, 41
discrimination, 95, 106
discontinuity
   excess of, 85
   at graduation, 56
   in an instruction system, 58
   in parallel systems, 81
   selection at each stage of, 86
   in a supervision system, 58
disciplinary measures, 57
discipline, 60
discipline-based departments, *see under* departments
discipline-based research, *see under* research
disequilibrium, 14
divinity, 75
doctorates, 75
dropouts, 56, 58

INDEX

education
　definition of, 24, 49–50, 61
　increased demand for higher level of, 21, 51, 56, 71, 86
　operating systems of, 42
　organizational model for task performance in, 41–55
　postgraduate, 25, 36, 71–80, 86
　primary, 86
　secondary, 86
　vocational, 73
educational process, dependent culture of, 88
educational processes, research into, 62
elite, intellectual, 51
elite universities, 5, 98
empire-building, 86
engineering, 73
enterprise
　boundaries, 17
　control and service functions of, 9
　conversion processes in, 7–8, 9, 12
　as an open system, 7–8, 13
environment
　constraints imposed by, 88
　of education, 61
　of an enterprise, 7, 8, 9, 13, 14, 17
　of a research unit, 40
　of a system of activities, 80
　of a university, 5, 103
equipment, 30, 31, 41, 96
experimental services, 83
explosion of knowledge, *see under* knowledge

faculty
　competence, 107
　control, 42
　councils, 83, 90
　discipline-based, 86
　discontinuity, 85
　heads, 46
　management, 46, 47, 50
　members, 52, 65, 82, 86, 97, 102, 107
　　junior, 89, 91, 93, 94
　senior, 90, 93, 94, 98, 105
　in model organizations, 64, 68, 83
　multiple-role carrying in, 64
　as operating system, 46
　and policy-making,
　power, 60, 66, 106
　and students, 42, 57, 91, 93, 99, 101
　and task-oriented sentient groups, 67
　tasks, 83
families, 57
family businesses, 14
finance, 29, 31, 37, 40, 67, 96
fragmentation and diversity, 78, 79, 80

generalist, the, 49, 78, 79, 97
generation gap, 99
goal
　boundaries, 12
　commitment, 52
　confusion, 36
government, the, and the university, 105
government research contracts, 72
graduates, 56, 58, 73, 82
graduation, 56, 58, 86
group dynamics, 62
groups
　reference, 5
　research, 85
　sentient, 13, 37, 39, 64, 66, 67, 68, 77, 91, 102
　working, 90, 91, 92, 95
growth and maturation
　definition of, 52
　opportunities for, 41, 50–5, 56, 57, 58, 59, 60, 61, 62, 74, 77, 81, 86, 87, 99

halls of residence, 60
health services, 79, 80
'helping' professions, 74
humanities, 35, 36, 72, 100, 101
human sciences, 35, 36

identification
　of faculty members with students, 61

identification *(cont.)*
  as inhibitor of innovation, 75
  in sentient groups, 31
  of student with teacher, 74
  of student with university community, 60, 65
imitation, 74, 75
impermeable boundaries, 40, 80
impersonalization, 60
import-conversion-export processes and systems, *see* conversion processes; *see under* system(s)
India, 1, 2, 3, 20, 22, 81, 103
Indian Education Commission, 2-3, 20-1, 23-4
individual performance, 95
innovation and change, 51, 61, 67, 75, 80, 90, 91, 94, 98, 102, 108
institutes of management, 75
institution, as an open system, 4
institutional commitment, 31, 52, 85
institutional culture, 85
institutional management, 31, 46, 66, 67, 68
institutional models of behaviour, 91
institution-building, 94
instruction
  as a primary task, 50, 56, 60
  in professional training, 73
  system, *see under* system(s)
intellectual elite, 51, 100
intellectual freedom, 94
intellectual training, 41, 49, 50, 56, 57, 58, 60
interdependence of tasks, *see under* task
investment decisions, 37, 40

job security, 94, 95

knowledge
  discovery and dissemination of, 56, 57, 77, 81, 105
  explosion of, 2, 21, 35, 47, 50, 71, 88
  integration of, 41
  new, 26, 28, 29, 36, 50, 72

leaders
  conflict between, 65
  university as producer of, 50
leadership
  adaptive, 102
  and change, 108
  and compromise, 103
  creative and innovative, 90, 95
  and dependent culture, 94
  inhibited by organization, 92
  institutionalized, 66
  of institutional management, 68
  in professional schools, 80
  in project-type organization, 33, 34
  roles, 50-51
  capacity to adopt, 82
  rehearsal of, 62
  of teachers, 42
  of university, 57, 106
learning, integration of, 47-50
liberal arts, the, 49
library, 67
'living' process, 53, 66, 78
'living' system, 60, 66

management
  control, 8, 30, 37, 42, 81
  faculty, 46, 47, 50
  institutes of, 75
  institutional, 31, 46, 66, 67, 68
  research-programme, 34
  research-unit, 31, 37
  roles, 34
  and specialization, 78
  task, 8
  of tutorial system, 53
  university, 3, 60, 87, 102
managing systems, *see under* system(s)
mathematics, 97
matriculates, 58, 82, 86
matriculation, 58
medical profession, 74, 79
medical research, 27
medical schools, 75, 78, 79, 80
Model Act (India), 103-4

INDEX

model-building, 3, 86, 88
model organization
  for professional schools, 76–80
  for task performance
    in education, 41–55
    in research, 26–40
  for undergraduate education, 56–70
  for a university, 81–7
models of behaviour, *see under* behaviour
motivated disorganization, 107
multiple role-carrying, 64, 65, 68, 82, 102
multiple routes, 68
multiple task systems, *see under* system(s)
multiple variables, 26, 27

natural sciences, 35, 36, 72, 101
Nehru, Jawaharlal, 20
nuclear physics, 72
numeracy, 49

objectives, of a university, *see under* university
office-holding, 95
open system, enterprise as, 7–8, 13
operating systems, *see under* system(s)
organization, system theory of, 3, 7–19
organizational boundaries, 12, 68, 82
organizational change, 5, 39
organizational chaos, 82
organizational compromise, 88
organizational models, *see under* model organization
organizations
  project, 15–16, 19, 30, 34, 35
  temporary and transitional, 15–16
over-determination, 55, 93, 95
over-identification, 55, 93
Oxford, University of, 66

participation
  in decision-making, 61, 88, 89–92
  management and, 68

postgraduate, 64
permissive culture, 51
personal conflict, 92
personal relationships, 82, 92
personal status, 82
personnel function, 67
planning and development function, 83
policy implementation, 89, 90
policy interpretation, 90
policy-making, 89, 90, 91
polytechnic, 73
postgraduate education, 25, 36, 71–80, 86
postgraduate research, 36, 37, 85
postgraduate students
  quality of, 82
  relationships of, with university community, 57, 77, 78
practice under supervision, 73, 75
presidency, 104
primary task
  concept of, 4
  definition of, 13
  of discipline-based departments, 36
  of an educational institute, 41
  of an enterprise, 7, 8, 9, 12
  of postgraduate departments, 36
  of a research institute, 31–3
  of sub-systems, 25
  of a tutorial system, 59
primary-task performance, *see under* model organization *and* task
primitive societies, 14
problem-centred research, 30–3, 37, 73
problem-centred research institutes, 35, 37, 39
problem-solving, 36, 40
process flow, 12
productivity, 41
professional bodies, 74
professional control, 27
professional practitioners, 82
professional schools, 76–7, 80, 83, 85
professional training, 56, 64, 71, 72, 73–80, 81, 85, 93

115

project groups, 15
project organizations, *see* organizations, project
project teams, 19, 30, 31, 37, 64
promotion, 94
protest, *see under* student
psychiatry, 62
'pure' science, 26, 73, 77

qualified practitioners, 73
qualifications, *see* degrees; diplomas; doctorates; status
quasi-autonomous research institutes, 39
quasi-autonomous states, 34
question formulation, 26

reality-testing, 93
reference groups, 5
regulation, 8
religious belief, 88, 100
Report of the committee on relations with junior members, 96
research
  action, 62
  applied, 26
  classification of, 26-8
  culture, 67
  departmental, 35
  discipline-based, 34, 35, 71
  equipment, 30, 31
  faculty, 75, 76, 79
  financial support for, 40
  groups, 85
  institutes, 64, 66, 71, 83, 85
  interdependence of, with teaching, 65
  management, 35, 37, 61
  matrix for, 26-7
  medical and social, 27
  methodology, 71, 73, 81
  multidisciplinary, 34, 35, 37, 39, 71
  organizational model for task performance in, 26-40
  organizational problems of, 71
  postgraduate, 64, 71-3, 80, 85
  problem-centred, 28, 30-3, 35, 37, 71
  problems, finding of, 71
  publication of, 27
  scientists as throughput of, 28-30
  standards, 86
  sub-systems of, 24
  traditional, 71
  tycoons, 37, 40, 64, 71, 73
  at undergraduate level, 59, 61-2
  university-based, model for, 37-40
  worker, 27, 30, 31, 36, 72
research-programme management, 33-4
research-unit management, 31
residential universities, 53, 59, 66
responsibilities, *see* authorities and responsibilities
Robbins Report, the, 103
role(s)
  adult, 59, 61, 62
  authority, 92
  behaviour, 65
  changes, 64
  competence, 82
  definition, 89
  differentiation, 60
  executive, 90
  identification, 5
  leadership, *see under* leadership
  multiple, 64, 68, 82, 102
  recognition, 66
  relationships, 12, 13, 14, 18, 29, 89, 92
  sets, 11

sanctions, 18
'schools', *see* professional schools
sciences
  applied, 101
    see also under research
  'basic', 39, 71
  biological, 35, 36, 72
  human, 35, 36
  natural, 35, 36, 72, 101
  'pure', 26, 73, 77
  social, 26, 72, 73, 100
scientific method, 28

INDEX

Scott, R. F., 99
selection procedures, 86
self-generated intakes, 40
self-generated questions, 40
senates, 90
sentient groups, *see under* groups
sentient systems, *see under* system(s)
service functions, *see* control and service functions
sinecures, 95
society, demands of, 98–100
Socrates, 99
specialist, the, 49, 78, 79, 97
specialization
    differentiated from research, 34–6, 71
    effects of, on students, 97
    excess of, 50, 59
    increase of, 39, 49, 78, 79
    and tutoring, 53
specific tasks and skills, 82
standards
    of inclusion and exclusion and graduation, 46
    of scholarship, 80, 82, 88, 100–1
status
    of degrees, 36
    of departmental heads, 91
    hierarchy, 39
    of operating systems, 67, 68
    systems, *see under* system(s)
strategic changes, 13
student
    behaviour, 53, 59
    council, 83
    counselling, 62
    disorders, 62
    growth and maturation, 49–55, 60, 61
    identification problems, 65, 66
    as a person, 52, 97
    protest, 1, 2, 21, 23, 57, 61, 62, 94
    as throughput of organization, 46, 47
    unions, 57
student-teacher relationship, 42, 74, 87
sub-institutions, 4
sub-projects, 34

sub-systems, 24, 80
supervision, 50, 52, 53, 58, 59
supervisor, 50, 58, 64
supervisory system, *see under* system(s)
system, definition of term, 8
system conflict, 13
system theory of organization, 3, 7–19
system(s)
    activity, 4, 5, 9, 80, 102
    closed, 4
    conversion, 41, 73
    instruction, 58
    'living', 60, 66
    managing
        in model for professional school, 77
        in model for undergraduate education, 66–70
        in model for university, 83
        in an organization, 9
        in research institutes, 64
    multiple-task, 13–14, 19, 37
    open, 7–8
    operating
        in an educational institution, 45, 46, 47
        in model for university, 83
        of an organization, 9
        in professional schools, 76, 78
        in research institutes, 31–3
        status of, 67, 68
    sentient
        boundaries of, *see under* boundaries
        coincidence of with task systems, 29, 34
        and compromise, 107
        in model for university, 81
        in research, 31
        in a small enterprise, 15
        theory of, 11
    status, 28
    supervisory, 58, 59, 77, 78, 81
    task
        boundaries of, *see under* boundaries
        coincidence of with sentient systems, 29, 34

systems, task (*cont.*)
 and compromise, 107
 definition of, 8
 temporary and transitional, 15–16
 transactional, 17–19
 teaching, 24, 58, 64, 81
 tutorial, 58–61, 66, 77, 81
 value, 76, 88
 'working', 60, 66

task
 boundaries, 12
 commitment, 29
 definition, 107
 differentiation, 60
 interdependence, 4, 25, 37, 108
 management, 8
 performance
  constraints on, 87, 88–101
  continuous assessment of, 96
  decisions about, 92
  effective, 11, 106, 108, 109
  organizational model for, 26–40, 41–55
  by university, 57
 system, *see under* system(s)
Tavistock Institute, 3
teacher, 42, 74, 50
teaching
 culture, 67
 effects of consultancy work on, 79
 for the professions, 73, 75, 76
 standards, 86
 system, *see under* system(s)
 tasks, 65
 techniques, 74, 98
technical college, 73, 87
temporary and transitional organizations, *see under* organizations
temporary and transitional task systems, *see under* system(s)
tenure, 88, 94–5
tradition, 39, 94, 95, 98
transactions, *see under* boundaries

trustee body, 105–6
tutor, 52, 53, 55, 59, 60, 64, 78
tutorial system, *see under* system(s)
tycoons, *see under* research

undergraduate
 colleges, 81
  see also colleges
 education, 24, 25, 73, 76, 78, 80
  activities of, 58–9
  model organization for, 56–70
 educational institution, model for, 62–6
 population, 85
 research, 59, 61–2
United Kingdom, 49, 60, 79, 103
United States, 49, 56–7, 72, 81
university
 affiliate, 81
 autonomy, 103, 104
 closed-system organization of, 4
 elite, 5, 98
 expansion, effects of, 59–61
 final authority, 105
 governance, 24, 31, 70, 97, 102–6
 management, 3, 60, 87, 102
 model organization for, 25, 81–7
 as a multiple-task institution, 4, 37, 81, 96, 108
 objectives, 20–5, 88, 105, 108
 policy, 66, 67, 68, 89, 91, 103, 105
 and professional education, 75, 80
 residential, 53, 59, 66
 size, 85–7

vice-chancellor, role of, 103–5
vice-chancellorate, 104, 105
vocational training, 73, 87

wardens, 59, 60
working groups, 90, 91, 92, 95
'working' process, 53, 66
'working' system, 60, 66